# When Will the Suffering End?

## A Biblical Perspective on Suffering

### SUZANNE STUCKY

Disclaimer notice:

Please note that the information contained within this book is for educational and encouragement purposes only. Every effort has been made to present accurate and reliable information. No warranties of any kind are declared or implied. The author and publisher assume no responsibility of any kind, including but not limited to errors, omissions, and inaccuracies. Readers acknowledge the author is not licensed to give legal, financial, medical, or professional advice. Please consult the appropriate licensed professional if needed. The content within this book has been derived from various sources. By reading this document, the reader agrees that under no circumstance is the author or publisher responsible for any losses, direct or indirect, which are incurred as a result of the use of the information contained within this document.

Cover design created using Canva

# PRAISE FOR *When Will the Suffering End?*
## A Biblical Perspective on Suffering

"From the soul of someone who lives with chronic pain and is also a believer, this book is a testament from the inside out. This topic is frequently not addressed in the protestant tradition because the emphasis is on the risen Christ; whereas in the Catholic tradition the suffering Christ is the central emphasis of worship. As a protestant, Stucky bravely and honestly confronts and exposes the all-to-often taboo on talking about the meaning of suffering. Like death, it is not an easy topic to contemplate. This book is a must-read for current or past practicing Christians who suffer and often blame or abandon God for God's seeming injustice."

**Dr. JoAnn M Baird,** Ed D, LMFT

"Suzanne's personal story is full of a gritty and raw resilience, tested and tried in the furnace of pain and affliction. As a believer, Suzanne has wrestled with her soul's most agonizing questions, ultimately submitting them to God as an act of trust in His sovereign majesty, all the while awaiting the miraculous healing that her heart longs to discover. As an author, Suzanne has invited readers to sojourn alongside her, finding a friend who encourages them to bring their sorrows to His throne. Desiring to see her own limping walk serve Him by encouraging others, she does not disappoint. Exploring the divine mysteries hidden within momentary sufferings, her writing cheers others onward toward a closer walk with Thee, culminating in His promise of a time when human suffering ends and a tear-free, pain-free eternity begins."

**Dr. Kristen Cummins,** EdD, Traumatology
Licensed Marriage and Family Therapist
Board-Certified Professional Christian Counselor
Board-Certified Professional Life Coach

"Why do Christians suffer? It is a question asked for centuries. I just lost a good friend to cancer. He died way too early. Why God, why? I have known Suzanne for over 25 years as her friend and former pastor. It is my honor to recommend her thoughts and writings on the topic of suffering. Needless to say, she has done her lifework and homework on the topic. Buckle in and be ready to be challenged."

**Dr. Jim Lee**, Pastor and Commercial Pilot

"This book is a gift to the Body of Christ. Not only has Suzanne provided accessible and solid biblical exegesis here, but she's done so in the service of helping people process the difficulties of suffering. But what makes the book so unique is that Suzanne weaves her exegetical work together with her soul work. She doesn't preach from afar about suffering. Rather, her personal health issues and how she deals with them validate what she says about suffering. This book is a biblically faithful, graciously personal, powerfully applicable guide in navigating the hard road of suffering."

**Dr. Earl Waggoner**, PhD
Dean, Professor of Theological Studies
School of Biblical & Theological Studies
College of Adult & Graduate Studies
Colorado Christian University

# Dedications and Acknowledgements

First and foremost, God is the one who put this book on my heart. Without the leading of the Holy Spirit and the sacrifice of Jesus, none of this would be possible. It may sound cliché, but it's true. Second, the love and support of my husband, Eric, and daughter, Taylor, have been invaluable. Both have listened to my cries and helped me up (literally and figuratively) when I felt like I could not carry on—in life and in the writing of this book. Eric, my soulmate and love of my life, thank you for putting me through graduate school to earn my Master of Arts in Biblical Studies. You have walked this journey with me, and you have never stopped believing in me. Taylor, I am so blessed to be your mom. Thank you for showing me what it means to bloom where I am planted. To my son-in-law Josh, your computer knowledge and helping hand have saved me more than once. And to my grandson, Landon, may you always keep Jesus close to your heart. I am grateful to my parents, Haig and Shaké, my sister, Kathy, and all the family and friends who have put up with my limitations and supported me in spite of my bad days—those who let me cry, and those who gave me a dose of reality.

I especially want to thank those without whom this book would not be possible. First, my professor, who became my mentor and now my friend, Russ Meek, your kindness, listening ear, leading, and advice have been an incredible encouragement. Your own books have been such an inspiration to me, and I am beyond grateful for your editing expertise in the creation of this book.

Taylor Lee, I could not have put this book together without your tireless efforts. Your revisions have made this a better book. I appreciate you more than words can ever express.

I also want to acknowledge Matt Aernie, although he is no longer with us, for the motivational and supportive role he played in getting this project started.

Finally, to all of you who read this book, I am thankful for the opportunity to share my message of suffering and faith. I pray that it will be an encouragement to you. For those who suffer, please know that you are not alone.

# Contents

# Introduction

Why me, Lord? When is this suffering going to end? Life is so hard! I do not want to suffer anymore. (Insert crying emoji here.) No one chooses to suffer. Many people can endure for a little while knowing that things will eventually get better, but what happens when we know that the suffering will not end? It will only get worse here on earth; but one day, God will remove all pain and suffering (Rom 8:18; Rev 21:4). That is a guarantee. Remembering this promise helps us to endure.

That being said, how do we reconcile our suffering with our faith in God? Why does He allow suffering? Do I believe that God can take away our pain? Yes, I do, but only if it is His will. Since He is able, it is difficult to understand why He would choose not to. Throughout this book, we will look at occasions where God allows suffering. As we choose to worship God in the midst of our challenges, we can know that He is using our circumstances to further His kingdom and to prepare us for eternity, even if we don't understand why. Whatever the reason for our trials, God is at work.

This is not meant to be a trite "God's got this" book. Suffering is real and dealing with it is hard. It has taken me decades to understand the place of trials in my time on earth. As you read this book, you will likely discover more about me and my ongoing health challenges than you ever wanted to know, but what I hope you will come to understand is that throughout all my suffering, I have never lost my faith in God, and you can keep yours too. I pray that you will find the encouragement to trust God and remain faithful.

One of the things I have learned is that life on earth is not about me. It is about God—His plan, His purpose, His timing, and His will. When I can remember that, my suffering feels purposeful. If God took away my suffering, which I would love, I would not have this testimony to share with you. How much stronger is my testimony that I do not need to be healed to have faith in Jesus? Maybe that is the purpose for my afflictions. Maybe suffering is part of what makes me useful to God (Eph 21:10).

My goal is to encourage you to believe and have faith in God in spite of the challenges of life. Our time on earth is short when compared to eternity, so we only need to endure for a little while. To quote my friend Russ, "Life's brevity can act as a comfort to those who experience intense suffering in this world. For, while their current situation is dire, they know that it will not last forever."[1] Our suffering will end when Jesus returns or calls us home. Trials remind us that this is not our home.

---

[1] Russell L. Meek, *Ecclesiastes: A Participatory Study Guide,* (Gonzales, FL: Energion Publications, 2013), 66.

# How To Use This Book

After introducing my story, each subsequent chapter of this book covers a different Bible passage. I have found strength in these snippets of Scripture, and I hope you will too. After I share a bit about the meaning and significance of each passage, you will find commentary that gives the background —"Setting the Scene"—of the particular book of the Bible, the overall meaning of the passage, and a discussion of the individual verses. These are followed by theological reflections, ways the passage points to Jesus, and ways to apply these Scriptures to your daily life. Last comes a section called "The Details" which you can choose to read if you want to dig into more specific information regarding the literary and historical context of these passages. Are you ready? Here we go!

# Chapter 1

## WHY WRITE ABOUT FAITH AND SUFFERING?

### My Story

Everybody suffers, and for each of us that suffering looks different.
For me, suffering takes on a very physical form. I have had multiple
progressive diseases for over forty years which started in my early
twenties. I was diagnosed first with a progressive peripheral
neuropathy called Charcot-Marie-Tooth (CMT) Disease (although it
has nothing to do with teeth). The peripheral nerves are the ones
outside the brain and spinal cord. In CMT, these peripheral nerves do
not function normally causing a wide range of symptoms (See
Appendix A for details), most notably loss of muscle, loss of some
feeling in my hands and feet, severe loss of balance, walking
difficulties, and loss of any control over my ankles, so my feet just
flop. My toes curl under, so I cannot grip to hold shoes on my feet.
As a result, I trip over my toes, fall and injure myself quite a bit.
Since I can't lift my ankles, my body has learned how to walk
differently by lifting my legs high from the hips, causing back and
hip issues from the abnormal gait.

Throughout this book, I reference how I used to be able to

dance in heels. Dancing is one of the things I miss the most. Fun fact: I'm Armenian, and Armenians love to dance. It's in our DNA. Leading traditional line dances brought me so much joy in my younger years, so losing that sense of freedom and connection to my friends, family, and culture has been hard for me. Over the years, I have come to accept CMT as part of my life, though I still cry and get frustrated. After all, I am human. Unfortunately, the nature of progressive diseases is that they keep getting worse. Such is the case with mine. It is now quite visible as I wear leg braces to help stabilize my ankles, I have a service dog to help me balance, and my hands are starting to look deformed from the loss of muscle.

About fifteen years ago, when more issues began to arise, I was diagnosed with Autonomic Dysfunction, also called Dysautonomia (Appendix D). The autonomic system controls involuntary bodily functions such as heart rate, blood pressure, digestion, and sweating. My symptoms include dizziness and lightheadedness, irregular heartbeat, low blood pressure, bladder issues, insufficient sweating which causes severe heat intolerance, and an internal itch so horrible that episodes last for months at a time, resulting in bleeding from scratching so hard, even in my sleep.

Next came the diagnosis of Sjogren's Disease (Appendix B). Test results and odd symptoms did not lead to a diagnosis for years. A visit to the Mayo Clinic finally confirmed Sjogren's. This is a chronic autoimmune disorder that primarily affects the moisture-producing glands, leading to dryness in various parts of the body. As a result, I have eight different issues with my eyes, abnormally dry skin, and ulcers in my mouth with literally every organ in my body at risk.

Most recently came the diagnosis of Ehlers-Danlos Syndrome (EDS) which is a group of connective tissue disorders (Appendix C). Connective tissue is what holds tissues, cells, and organs together, giving the body its shape. Blood, bone, cartilage, tendons, and ligaments are all connective tissue. My symptoms include joint hypermobility, scoliosis, skin that bruises very easily, joint pain, slight mitral valve prolapse, and an aortic aneurysm. Joint hypermobility causes dislocations, sprains, and pain with my worst symptom being that my ribs slip out of place which can make breathing difficult and can be excruciatingly painful. Additionally, my venous insufficiency leaves my leg veins weak, so instead of pumping blood back to my heart effectively, blood pools in my ankles.

Outside of the main progressive diseases above, I have more minor issues like Hashimoto's hypothyroidism, rosacea, dermatographia (skin writing), arthritis, severe osteopenia (which is not good for someone who falls), and a bunch of other less severe ailments. I am not telling you this so that you'll feel sorry for me. You may not even define my experience as true suffering. I am not trying to discount anyone else's suffering. I am sharing my story to convey to you that, for me, I understand what it means to suffer. For the most part, I have learned to live with my diagnoses, although I grieve each new loss as things progress. What I want to communicate is that my suffering serves a purpose in God's plan, and I have faith even in the worst of my suffering.

Suffering comes in many forms, not just physical health problems. You may relate to my specific form of suffering, or you may not, and that is okay. All these passages can be applied to your specific hardship. Let's dig into Scripture as I explain more.

# Chapter 2

## WHY DOES GOD ALLOW SUFFERING?

### Job 42:2–6

*"I know that you can do all things;*
*no purpose of yours can be thwarted.*
*You asked, 'Who is this that obscures my plans*
*without knowledge?'*
*Surely I spoke of things I did not understand,*
*things too wonderful for me to know.*
*"You said, 'Listen now, and I will speak;*
*I will question you, and you shall answer me.'*
*My ears had heard of you*
*but now my eyes have seen you.*
*Therefore I despise myself and repent*
*in dust and ashes."* (NIV)

A classic suffering passage seems like a good place to start this book. Many think of Job when they think of unjust suffering. He experienced one problem on top of another. Have you ever heard someone say, "I feel like Job"? I can relate. Every time I go to a doctor, I get a new diagnosis or hear that one of my many diseases is getting worse. Seriously? Again? And it just keeps getting worse. I definitely feel like Job with one disease stacking on top of the next! When will it end? But when it comes to the ways of God, who am I to question Him? What do I know? In my finite mind, suffering is for the wicked. I mean, I am a fairly good person in the scheme of humanity (in my own humble assessment!), so why am I suffering? Meanwhile, I'm watching bad people (according to my definition) thrive. Is God mean? What did I do to deserve so many health struggles?

For me, suffering affects just about every part of my body. My health declines in spite of how hard I fight to hold onto the strength I have. No fair! While most people work out and keep getting stronger, I spend hours each day exercising and doing physical therapy, but I get worse anyway. I miss out on things because of my lack of physical abilities, not to mention the emotional aspects of declining health (more on that in Chapter 5). I share this with you to make the point that when I question God on why I suffer with these health issues, I am speaking about things I know nothing about. I know that God can handle my moaning, crying, and frustration—in fact, He welcomes them—but ultimately I must trust His authority. But how? It's not as if I can calm myself down knowing that my pain is temporary. There is no end in sight, no control over my circumstances, and no one who can make it better for me. I can stay stuck there, but it is nothing more than frustrating and discouraging. God gives and God can take away. People say that life is not fair, but have you ever thought that other people compare themselves to you? Is it fair that you and I have what we have? Is it fair that some other "good" person has it worse than we do? And what about Jesus? Is it fair that He suffered for our sins? If life was fair, we would be the ones on that cross, not Jesus. (Imagine, God watched His only begotten Son suffer beyond all comprehension when He died on the cross to reconcile us to God. As a parent, that would be too much for me to bear.) On the surface, the answer is no, it's not fair, but life is not about fairness. It is about God—His plan, His purpose, and His authority.

## Setting the Scene

As we look at the story of Job, let's begin with the moral of the story. It takes forty-two chapters to get there, but in one sentence, God is sovereign. Job was a righteous man who worshiped God. He had everything—wealth, prosperity, family, health, status, and faith in God. Satan believed that Job was only faithful to God because of his immense success, so he challenged Job's loyalty by asking God to allow him to afflict Job. Knowing Job's devoted heart, God agreed, and Job faced one loss after another until everything was gone, including his health. Job's friends came to comfort him, but instead they insisted that his suffering was the result of his own sin and they urged him to repent. Job knew he had done nothing wrong, but when he questioned his unjust misery, God essentially told Job that he was not there when God made His plans and created everything, so he could not possibly begin to understand God's ways. Eventually, Job repented of his questioning and acknowledged that God is right— humans cannot possibly grasp God's authority and grace. Job ultimately recognized his unworthiness and that he had spoken about things he did not understand (42:3).

Although Job could not explain the reason for his suffering, the Book of Job offers a biblical perspective on suffering. This book asks whether or not God is just. If Job is suffering as a righteous and blameless man, does God run the world on the principle of justice? Romans 12:19 says that vengeance belongs to God, meaning that it is not our place to seek revenge because He will be the one to judge. This concept emphasizes God's justice, so there must be another explanation for Job's seemingly unjust suffering. In Job's confusion about how a good God can allow a blameless person to suffer, he questions God. It is the same question that plagues us as believers today. The concept that the good should prosper and the bad should suffer lays the groundwork for the book of Job. This is called retribution theology. In the days of Job, Genesis, and wisdom literature in general, retribution theology was a real expectation. It is even spelled out throughout the Bible. Exodus 21:23–25 states, "if there is serious injury, you are to take life for life, eye for eye, tooth for tooth, hand for hand, foot for foot, burn for burn, wound for wound, bruise for bruise" (NIV). That is, punishment should be related to the level of the wrongdoing committed. Galatians 6:7 says, "A man reaps what he sows," showing that individuals are responsible for what they receive in life.

The book of Job confuses us because it feels as though it leaves our questions about good people suffering unanswered, but the truth is that Job's wrestling leads him to a greater comprehension of God's wisdom and goodness. It is through our search to understand suffering that our lives may be changed as we learn to persevere in faith in all circumstances.

The main ideas in the book of Job are that 1) suffering comes according to God's mysterious reasons, and 2) God's wisdom is beyond anything we can ever fathom. The purpose of Job is to examine God's guidelines about fairness, but we cannot ever truly obtain enough evidence to properly achieve this. Rather, "his justice must be inferred from his wisdom,"[2] which is far greater than human wisdom.

# Overall Meaning of the Passage

Wisdom is the knowledge of how things work, and it implies good judgment. For Job, this includes living his best life despite his horrific circumstances, but, can Job reconcile what he knows of God with his intense suffering? Job fears God, but he does not have the wisdom to understand why he suffers. In his view, his suffering results from God's unjust treatment (Job 9:17–19; 16:6–17; 19:7–12, 21).[3] He is stuck between the reality of his circumstances and his understanding of God's character. Job's doubts come because "the evidence of his eyes tells him that God is dangerous, random, and unpredictable. The faith in his heart tells him that God is righteous and that he is a believer who is in the right before God . . . despite the evidence of randomness and danger."[4] He oscillates between faith

<hr>

[2] Andrew E. Hill, and John H. Walton, *A Survey of the Old Testament* (Grand Rapids, MI: Zondervan Academic, 2009), 401.

[3] JiSeong J. Kwon, "Meaning and Context in Job and Tobit," *Journal for the Study of the Old Testament* 43, no. 4 (2019): 635.

[4] Brian P. Gault, "Job's Hope: Redeemer or Retribution?" *Bibliotheca Sacra* 173, no. 690 (2016): 148.

and challenging God. It is his faith that causes Job to challenge God. Job laments, grieves, and complains in his misery, but he brings his suffering to God (7:11). He makes sure that God knows that he is being treated unjustly (10:3) because he knows that God can make things right. God seems to be the problem and the solution.[5] The first time God responds to Job's cries, He says, "Who is this that obscures my plans with words without knowledge? . . . "Where were you when I laid the earth's foundation?" (38:2,4 NIV).  Here God points out Job's limited outlook and claims His authority over all creation. After wrestling with God and His role in suffering, Job comes to understand that God can do all things. God is not required to *only* bless the righteous without any suffering (John 9:2–3). He concedes that he now understands and that before he spoke with limited knowledge about how God runs the world.

This repentance is the correct response for Job, but if he is innocent, what is he repenting of? He apologizes for cursing the day of his birth, his longing to die, his despair, his arrogance, his complaints against and challenges to God, and for speaking about things of which he knows nothing. He had not sinned by relenting to his friends' accusations and falsely agreeing with them; rather, his repentance includes his attitude and own words during his ordeal. It was not sin that caused his suffering, so there was no need to repent of some earlier sin. This realization allows Job to move past his frustration. Once Job repents for speaking of things he knows nothing about and questioning God's wisdom, God restores his

---

[5] William Leland Kynes, and William Joseph Kynes, *Wrestling with Job* (Downers Grove, IL: InterVarsity Press, 2022), 98.

health, then doubles his success, family, and wealth.

Rather than expecting fairness, Job calls us to submit "to the mysteries of God's world…. Like us, Job does not need to know more; rather, he needs to learn a humble and yet intimate relationship with God that enables him to embrace his creatureliness."[6] Did you catch that? This is the solution to enduring suffering on earth—to "submit to the mysteries of God's world." We do not need to know why we suffer. Although we always want answers, the remedy is to accept our circumstances and trust God's plan. In God's divine design, unjust suffering is a part of His plan to make things right again. Eventually Job recognizes that God can and will use this suffering for His godly purposes.

With Job's humble submission to God, Satan's accusations of Job's false loyalty are proven untrue. Job's faith in God has prevailed. Through God's allowance of Job's suffering, He provides comfort for Job and all those sufferers yet to come (2 Cor 1:4). That's you and me!

## Discussion of Individual Verses

**Job 42:2:** *"I know that you can do all things; no purpose of yours can be thwarted."*

Here, Job comes to realize that there is nothing God cannot do. God is omnipotent (all-powerful), and whatever He wants is what will

---

[6] Craig G. Bartholomew, and Ryan P. O'Dowd, *Old Testament Wisdom Literature: A Theological Introduction* (Downers Grove, IL: IVP Academic, 2011), 149.

happen (Matt 19:26; Dan 4:35) for His good purposes. Nothing can derail God's plans. God can turn Job's intense suffering into good, and He will at the end of time. This gives Job the strength to endure. He realizes that universal judgment does not belong to humans. As Job expresses his assumption about God and his own lack of knowledge, he recognizes that in God's ability to "do everything," God could also comfort Job and assure him of His presence. God explains that if He can control the evil creatures, Behemoth and Leviathan (chs. 40–41), then He can certainly manage Job's life. God's wisdom and justice reign.

**Job 42:3:** *"You asked, 'Who is this that obscures my plans without knowledge?' Surely I spoke of things I did not understand, things too wonderful for me to know."*

**"You asked, 'Who is this that obscures my plans without knowledge?'"** God's question to Job refers back to the similar questions He asked Job earlier in 38:3 and 40:7. It is more of a rhetorical question to remind Job of God's sovereignty.

**"Surely I spoke of things I did not understand, things too wonderful for me to know."** Job admits his pride, ignorance, and lack of understanding about God's design for creation. This stresses his new awareness of his finite understanding in comparison to God's infinite wisdom. Since Job cannot even comprehend the natural world (chs. 38–41), he cannot begin to preach about a righteous world or instruct God about anything. Instead, Job could learn from the suffering God allowed in his life. In his most intense anguish, Job said things he now regrets because he doubted the goodness of God and the fairness of His judgment. Here, he returns to his previous state of satisfaction, leaving things in God's hands (cf. Ps 131). Through his negative description of his own wisdom, Job affirms the wisdom of God.[7] This new insight confirms that the classical retribution theory of Proverbs may have been misunderstood. As Job recognizes his own limitations, he is showing that he understands the point of God's speeches. He recognizes the complexity of the universe and that he will never understand the mysteries of God. Job agrees with God that he was guilty and spoke about things that were beyond his ability to comprehend. In faith, Job acknowledges that God is true to justice in His authority over the cosmos.

**Job 42:4:** *"You said, 'Listen now, and I will speak; I will question you, and you shall answer me.'"*
**"You said"** recalls God's words from his first speech (38:3).
**"'Listen now, and I will speak; I will question you, and you shall answer me.'"** Job knows he is unable to answer any of God's questions. Here, Job stops challenging God (31:35–40) and instead asks God if he may speak. This is where Job shifts his understanding and interaction with God. This verse shows the importance of communicating with God. Since Job is willing to have a mutual exchange with God, he proves his humility, faith, and need to connect with God. Actively bringing laments, concerns, and

---

<sup>7</sup> Kwon, "Meaning and Context in Job and Tobit," 634.

questions to God as well as listening for His reply is important in our relationship with God, but ultimately, we have to trust His ways. Job admits that his search for the wisdom to explain his suffering can never be answered because the wisdom of God exceeds his own understanding.

**Job 42:5:** *"My ears had heard of you but now my eyes have seen you."*

***"My ears had heard of you."*** This "hearing" is to understand in an intellectual way.

***"My eyes have seen you."*** This statement does not imply that Job saw a vision. He is simply saying that this experience with God is real and personal. "Seeing God" is a metaphor for God's presence. God is not hidden. In the past Job's knowledge of God was only what he had heard (God's message), but now it is a genuine firsthand experience. As Job reflects on his previous obliviousness, his thinking undergoes a transformation. Through his encounter with God, Job can now see that his understanding is limited. This is an essential feature of faith. "Seeing" God is not a literal sense of the word, rather it is knowing that God is with us in our troubles. It is having a real and personal relationship with God as opposed to simply "hearing."

Job's deepest desire to see his Redeemer (Savior, Defender) with his own eyes is fulfilled (19:25–27). In his state of awe, Job's complaints seem insignificant. Job had referred to God hiding (23:8–9), and He is no longer hidden. In Job 19:25–27, Job's desire to see

God was clear, so now that he has a better perspective after talking to God, he says his "eyes have seen" God. This is a furthering of Job's belief in God's presence and immeasurable wisdom. The most important aspect of being in relationship with God is simply loving Him and abiding in His presence. Knowing God is more valuable than knowing all the answers.

**Job 42:6:** *"Therefore I despise myself and repent in dust and ashes"* Scholars consider this verse to be the most significant passage in the Book of Job.

*"I despise myself."* Job repents in humility with this statement. This could be translated as "I reject what I said," withdrawing his previous uninformed statements, foolish words, and accusations against God for treating him unfairly.

*"Repent in dust and ashes."* Sitting in ashes and wearing sackcloth was a physical sign of mourning or showing remorse in Job's day. Job is sorry for what he said and mourns his foolish statements. While Job never loses his faith in God, after confronting Him, Job changes directions in his thinking. This shift comes from his interaction with and understanding of God. He is not saying that his complaints were unfounded; rather, he now realizes that they are no longer proper. Although Job's questions have not been answered, Job comes to understand that God, not Job, is in control. This realization strengthens Job's faith. After all, humankind is formed from dust from the ground (Gen 2:7) and will return to dust (Gen 3:19), meaning that the wisdom of people can never compare to that of the

God who created humanity. This indicates that we will always be limited in our understanding of suffering.

# Theological Reflections

Theological themes in the book of Job include the character of God, faith, retribution theology, and the meaning of human suffering. Let's take a look at each theme:

*Character of God:* Job knows the character of God to be holy (6:10), wise (9:4; 12:13), and all-powerful (6:14), allowing Him to do as He pleases (23:13). God is all-knowing and all-seeing (28:24), the creator of constellations (9:7–8) and humanity (10:8–12; 31:15). Job also knows that God is sovereign (12:15, 23; 14:5), forgiving (14:16–17), and can do things that no human mind can comprehend (9:10). Job also believes God to be a merciful judge (9:15).

*Faith:* Job proves his faith through his unwavering loyalty to God despite immeasurable suffering. Faith tells Job that God is good and He is in control, so he says, "The Lord gives and the Lord takes away; blessed be the name of the Lord" (1:21). Through all his loss, Job maintains his trust in God. When Job's wife suggests that he "curse God and die" (2:9 NIV), Job tells her she is being foolish and acknowledges that God gives both good and trouble (2:10). He continues to have faith in God's good purpose.

*Retribution Theology*: Job 42:2–6 explains that humanity misunderstands and misapplies retribution theology. The concept that the righteous are rewarded and the wicked are punished is similar to the covenant in Deuteronomy that says that blessing and curses for

Israel are correlated with obedience or disobedience to God (Deut 28). Our misunderstanding is that retribution comes in this life. This is faulty theology. Job questions God because he cannot reconcile God's goodness as he knows it with the suffering he is experiencing. God teaches Job that suffering is not just the result of sin, and Job comes to realize that true justice is up to God and is not guaranteed while on earth. This is accurate theology.

*Meaning of human suffering*: Job 42:2-6 is the theological crux of the book. While retribution theology was a strongly held theological belief, it does not always explain suffering. We, and Job's friends, want everything to fit into a neat little box, but innocent suffering does not fit into that box. Like Job, we tend to complain about unjust suffering. God can handle our complaints, but, we would be mistaken to think that suffering is senseless or without purpose.

There is a poem called "Life is but a Weaving" (written by Grant Tullar but made famous by Corrie ten Boom) whose main idea is that life is like a tapestry. We see the underside with all the ugly knots and hanging threads, but God sees the upper side as He weaves together a beautiful picture. We cannot see the upper side from down here, so we cannot begin to understand the complete design God has planned; therefore, we need to trust that God is weaving something magnificent. Our suffering is part of what makes the tapestry beautiful.

Suffering reveals our desperate need for God. Here we come to understand that the message of Job is not so much about our actual suffering; rather it is about our relationship with God. When we can accept our suffering, we may even see it as God's grace toward us, drawing us closer to Him as it reveals God's true nature. Just recently, I came to understand that same act of grace in my own life, and through it I drew closer to God. He chose me for the particular purpose of sharing my story to encourage you in your faith. In my suffering, limping, weakness, and all the rest of it, this is how I am able to serve Him. I know that sounds a little crazy. I mean, who would want to suffer? God has chosen each of His children to fulfill a certain role, and mine is to encourage you. When I look at it from that perspective, I see it as a blessing.

Throughout history, Job's name has become synonymous with patience and humility. Years later, James refers to Job's steadfastness and faithfulness under trials in the New Testament (Jas 1:12; 5:11). Rather than answering our questions, the focus is put on God who has all the answers—whether or not He chooses to share those answers with us. The basis of Christian theology has not changed over time. It is to worship God and trust Him and His purposes.

## Pointing to Jesus

Our confession in the resurrecting power of Christ is paramount to our ultimate retribution and salvation. On this side of the cross, we can see that the Book of Job points to Jesus (16:19–21; 19:25–27). Jesus suffered immensely, incurring great torture, but upon His resurrection, God's purpose was revealed. This was the only way for God to save humanity. Jesus's suffering is part of God's plan, and so is ours. It occurs to me that my suffering may be accomplishing part of God's plan too. What if the only way for God to weave everything together includes our suffering? Just as we need faith in Jesus for our salvation, we need faith to accept that our misery is part of that very same plan.

Job understands that he has a redeemer (19:25) who is his final restoration. And so do we. The only answer is found in the gospel of Jesus Christ. Jesus experienced suffering on earth just as we do. Although He was blameless, Jesus suffered on the cross so that we would not have to. His death took on our ultimate suffering (eternity without God). In the meantime, we will continue to suffer on earth, making a book like Job necessary.

Like Job, Jesus is the innocent sufferer; and like Job, He also cried out in His agony on the cross (Matt 27:46). Just like Jesus, Job, in the midst of his suffering, intercedes for his unrighteous friends in order to reconcile them to God. We are like those unrighteous friends when we mistakenly believe that suffering is always the direct consequence of our sin instead of a more complicated reality.

Job 26 reveals that Job expects to see God, hinting at his recognition of the coming of the new heaven and earth (Job 14:12; Heb 1:10–12). It is through this faith that we are united with Christ and share in His everlasting fate.

The story of Job is a precursor to the story of Jesus. Like Job, Christ shows us how we are to live and how God created humanity in the first place. Jesus is the mystery of God (Col 2:2–3), and He embodies the wisdom of God. Jesus never sinned, yet in His righteousness and perfection He suffered immeasurably to reconcile us to God forever. Sometimes there is no explanation for suffering. Like Job, we may suffer because of our righteousness, and there is blessing in that (Matt 5:10). Things in the here and now are temporary—good and bad, joy and suffering. They all fade away when we look to Jesus. In other words, "our light and momentary troubles are achieving for us an eternal glory that far outweighs them all" (2 Cor 4:17 NIV). Even when we think God has abandoned us, He is always there. His love for us is shown through the life, death, and resurrection of Jesus which is the ultimate display of God's unfailing love.

# Application

My friend and I have a joke that if we ran the world, it would be a better place. The truth is, we are not equipped to run the world, nor can we see things from God's perspective. Just as Job realizes that his knowledge and understanding are incomplete, we recognize that we will never have the wisdom and power of God. It is our role to humbly submit to God's sovereignty, knowing that His ways are higher than ours. Scripture promises us trials and suffering in this world (John 16:33). Suffering deepens faith. We were never promised that things would be easy. Recovery may not happen the way we want or at all, so we get frustrated, but God is faithful in the midst of our suffering. He can do anything.

When life is good, we tend to forget God and lose our ability to be a good witness for Him. Others see God when they watch us endure trials faithfully. True faith believes no matter what. God does not waste anything. He has a purpose for everything. When the distance between our suffering and His promises is great, we need to pray. He welcomes our questions and laments. He knows it is hard, but He wants us to depend on Him.

We know that God's plans are for our good because the Bible tells us so in Romans 8:28: "And we know that in all things God works for the good of those who love him, who have been called according to his purpose" (NIV). It can be difficult to view our suffering as "for our good," but this passage displays God's plan of redemption for His people. "Good" is defined in God's terms whereas we tend to incorrectly define "good" as success, wealth, and health. Rather, God will work all things for "good" by turning our current suffering into future glory which is our transformation to the image of Christ and sharing in His glory in heaven. It is through our trials that we grow, allowing us to develop our faith and character. Our character, our love for others, and our relationship with God are the only things we take with us to heaven. That sounds pretty important.

Trials come in many forms—relationships, finances, and health to name a few. Job experienced all of them at once. Through his suffering, Job came to recognize God's supremacy and that we do not need to be ruled by our circumstances. When I can remember that, I realize that my suffering is part of God's plan. His will can be accomplished through my suffering. Nothing in God's plan is inconsequential or without reason.

Job 42:2–6 is the key to understanding suffering: We are to trust God's sovereignty and goodness in the midst of our suffering even though it does not make sense to us. This is not easy. Sometimes it is a moment-by-moment decision. Sometimes we flip-flop between trust and doubt. That's okay. God understands. The Book of Job shows us that God has His mysterious reasons for what He does, and His wisdom far surpasses anything we could ever even begin to comprehend. God may or may not restore us here on earth—like He did Job—but you can count on full restoration in heaven. What a comforting thought. We do not need to have all the answers. In other words, we do not need to know why we suffer. We just need to trust that God is control. And ultimately, the more time we spend choosing faith, the more peace, acceptance, and joy we will have in our lives.

The ministry that God has placed on my heart is to help those who are suffering to have faith in Him. My hope is that you can relate my story to your own story of suffering. Just like Job, I am trying to make sense of unjust suffering. Mine is a grief that will not reach resolution in this life. Job 42:2–6 reminds us of the importance of humility, repentance, and trusting God and His plan. Job also teaches us that it is acceptable to turn to God with our laments, frustration, and questions. I do this often. Though it may be difficult at times, I eventually remember to trust Him and His plan for my life. It is in the highly intense seasons of suffering that we need Him the most. Every time my suffering intensifies, I seek God (after a good cry and lots of chocolate), and, like Job, my relationship with Him deepens as I learn to trust His sovereignty and wisdom. That is the blessing in the suffering. The only way we can line up our lives with God's perfect plan is by trusting in His wisdom and authority.

We certainly cannot do it on our own, nor were we meant to. To accomplish this, we must seek His direction through prayer, studying Scripture, and following the leading of the Holy Spirit. If we are willing to humble ourselves to hear His message, His wisdom will guide us.

Today, we struggle with the same questions and concerns as Job did, but God is not under any obligation to answer. The only solution is to accept suffering as part of God's sovereign plan. It has been said that "If God was small enough to be understood, he wouldn't be big enough to be worshiped."[8] Job's ultimate goal is to be in relationship with God (Ps 27:4) and to believe that God is good. In his pain, he still states that his "Redeemer lives" (19:25). His faith cannot be overcome.

Although it may appear that God is silent, He is always at work. I would love to get a peek at God's playbook, but that is not His will. Life on earth is about our relationship with God. Faith picks up where explanation stops. It says, "I trust you to handle this God." We must ask ourselves if we trust God, even in the midst of our suffering. "God is indeed good, and his purposes will be accomplished in the end; but this journey must be lived by embracing the mystery and wonder of human life in this world."[9]

Just as Job realizes that suffering serves as a refining process, suffering continues to bring me closer to God as I learn to trust Him more and more. I know that sounds counterintuitive, but if I do not

---

[8] As quoted in Timothy Keller, *Walking with God Through Pain and Suffering* (New York: Penguin, 2013), 255.

[9] Bartholomew and O'Dowd, *Old Testament Wisdom Literature*, 155.

trust Him in my suffering, I will fall deep into despair. It is only in knowing that my suffering serves His purposes that I can find peace. When God chooses us to suffer for His purposes, it is actually a compliment that He trusts us to be His hands and feet here on earth. It is not about you or me. It is about God. God is sovereign and we do not need to know any more than what He shows us. We only need to live in relationship with Him, trusting His wisdom, and waiting for the day when Christ returns to end our suffering. May we, like Job, find peace and clarity in surrendering ourselves to the wisdom and power of our Creator.

Job teaches us that: (1) Sometimes there is no explanation for suffering; (2) We must trust God's plan even when we do not understand; and (3) We must endure in faithfulness even in the face of trials. The happy ending of the story is that the righteous will be rewarded with the greatest prize of all time—Christ and eternity in heaven (Rom 8:18).

# The Details

## Literary and Historical Context

**Author:** The author of the Book of Job is unknown, so the assumption is that the writer is irrelevant to the message.

**Date:** Since the author cannot be determined, it is also difficult to definitively determine the time period during which Job was written, indicating its irrelevancy as well. The message is timeless making it more important than the author and date; however, scholars have speculated various dates for the writing. A patriarchal time period, most notably the time of Abraham, Isaac, and Jacob, has been suggested; however, the book does not refer to "the land of Israel, the priesthood, and the temple as would be typical for a patriarchal timeframe. But it was still connected to the Israelite faith—with its insistence on the justice of God."[10] The entire Pentateuch (the first five books of the Bible) and the Old Testament Historical Books go back and forth between Israel's faithfulness with resulting success and rebellion accompanied by anguish, so the book of Job is fitting in this context. One indicator for patriarchal times is the life of Job himself. He (1) lived at a time when fortune was determined by the number of animals one owned (1:3); (2) he was still offering sacrifices (1:5); and (3) he was famous in his day as a man of great righteousness (Ezek 14:14, 20; Jas 5:11).[11]

---

[10] Kynes and Kynes, *Wrestling with Job*, 7.

[11] Chad Brand, ed., *Holman Illustrated Bible Dictionary* (Nashville,: B&H, 2015), 903.

Other indicators point to a writing in the time of Solomon (970– 931 BC) since the book assumes the individual retribution theology found in the book of Proverbs.[12] Some consider dating the book after the reign of Hezekiah, who died around 686 BC, which was before the exile when the Jews were forced from their homeland into Babylonian captivity. Since the book alludes to Isaiah, Jeremiah, and Psalms, others would place a date after the exile; however, "the issue of suffering in the exile is that of national suffering caused by Israel's sin (e.g., Lamentations), but in Job, the issue is undeserved suffering of a righteous person."[13]

**Historical Time and Background:** Job lived in Uz which likely bordered Edom in the northern part of Arabia. The Edomites (descending from Isaac's son, Esau) were not viewed as good people.

More important than the exact location of the story is that it is not located in Israel. The land of Uz is included in a list of nations outside Israel (Jer 25:19–26). Job was identified as a human being, not specifically as an Edomite, making his plight more common to all of humanity. Either way, the location and timing of the book is not relevant to the book's message.

**Literary Background:** The first Jewish reference to the book of Job comes from the Septuagint, the Greek translation of the earlier ancient Hebrew manuscript. Since the Book of Job is theologically more similar to the Greek translation than the

---

[12] Lindsay Wilson, *Job*, Two Horizons Old Testament Commentary (Grand Rapids: Eerdmans, 2015), 14.

[13] Ibid., 12–13.

Hebrew version, it is thought that Job may have originated from Greek-speaking Alexandrian Jews.[14] The book also shows similarities with other ancient Near Eastern texts, and some see a similarity with Egyptian poems.[15] Certain scholars believe that parts of the book may have been added later—Elihu's speeches (32–37), Job's Hymn to Wisdom (28), and God's second speech (40:6–41:34), as well as "the prose prologue and epilogue, which are often presented as adopted from an ancient Epic of Job;"[16] however, all parts are necessary for the book to fully realize its purpose. Job contributes to the canon with its deep theology and tradition of Israelite wisdom, addressing the mystery of suffering. The book explores humanity's relationship with God and teaches about the righteousness of God.

**Genre and Literary Style:** Job is typically classified as wisdom literature, but it is different from the wisdom in Proverbs. The book includes narrative (1–2), soliloquy (3), dialogue (4–27), hymn (28), and discourse (29–41).[17] There is no other book like it. While Job is considered Narrative Wisdom, telling about the suffering of one man, his faith, and the mysteries of God, Proverbs offers advice and teaches how to live a righteous everyday life. Job has also been considered a historical story of actual events in the ancient Near East, a hypothetical story or parable for the sake of making a point, poetry, lawsuit drama,

---

[14] Stephen J. Vicchio, *The Book of Job: A History of Interpretation and a Commentary* (Eugene, OR: Wipf & Stock, 2020), Part I: The History of Interpreting the Book of Job.

[15] Brand, *Holman*, 904.

[16] Hill and Walton, *A Survey of the Old Testament*, 403.

[17] Ibid., 405.

and  skeptical literature.[18] Poems relating to the origin and development of the universe as well as "myths were a common way for ancient Near Eastern societies to understand and counter these situations; the appeal for justice is an appeal about the world order."[19]

**Biblical Context:** Job can be read in terms of biblical theology based on the entire Bible since retribution theology permeates the Bible. Job's place in the canon is as the picture of true faith. It raises the question of how to have faith in the midst of suffering, especially unjust suffering. Righteousness is not always rewarded, and evil is not always punished. It is not a straightforward formula. But true to the canon of Scripture, God prevails even in unjust circumstances. The Book of Job declares God's sovereignty. In the end, Job concludes that faith in God is the true value of life.

---

[18] Wilson, *Job*,  14.

[19] Bartholomew and O'Dowd, *Old Testament Wisdom Literature*, 136.

*Chapter 3*

## WHERE IS OUR HOME?

### Psalm 46:10

*He says, "Be still, and know that I am God;*
*I will be exalted among the nations,*
*I will be exalted in the earth." (NIV)*

We live in difficult times. We are constantly worried and busy. Anxiety is at an all-time high. And that is just daily, normal life. When you add suffering that does not end, it becomes difficult to find any peace at all. We all want to live a peaceful and joyful life. I am happiest and most at peace at home under a fuzzy blanket watching the snow fall. It brings me joy and comfort. In that moment, I get to forget that I have four chronic progressive diseases and various other health issues. Once I stand up, I am quickly reminded by the lightheadedness, strange heartbeat, weak hands, and awkward limp. The question is how to hold onto that peaceful feeling when I am not under the serenity of that blanket. Peace is in that feeling of being home, but this is not our home. "We feel that longing to come home, to seek refuge in a place of peace where we can truly feel at home, at rest, deep in our hearts. So if we are still unable to say to ourselves, 'I am at home, right here and now,' then this is an invitation for us to consider these questions: 'Where is my home? How can I find it? Where can I seek refuge?'"[20] Psalm 46 reminds us that "God is our refuge" (46:1) and heaven is our home. My friend says we are living in the reality of duality. Think about that. We know that heaven is our home, but we still live here on earth. We're going to suffer. That is a promise (John 16:33; Acts 14:22). It is the reality of living here. The other reality is that there will be no more suffering one day (Rev 21:4). This is the source of true joy. In the meantime, we live in the duality of two opposing worlds. We are allowed to be sad, angry, and frustrated. When our trials will not end in this life, we hold onto the reality that it is just for now.

Peace does not come from having more, doing more, buying things, striving to achieve, being more popular, being more successful, or being better. Actually, the opposite is true. The more we have, the more problems seem to follow. Eventually, we become dissatisfied. If this is not our home, why do these things matter? We will never have peace and joy until we can rest and "be still" in the presence of God. Let God do His thing. Our part is to *be still and know.*" But what does that mean? To "be still" means to stop struggling, quiet your mind, and surrender your circumstances. More than a physical stillness, it is a conscious decision to let go of control

---

[20] Ruben Habito, *Be Still and Know: Zen and the Bible* (Maryknoll, NY: Orbis, 2017), ch. 1.

in exchange for the inner peace that comes from trusting God and His outcome. This does not mean that we ignore our problems, rather we give our worries to God and let go of the results, knowing that He is in control, undisturbed in the midst of it all.

As one with quality-of-life progressive health issues, I can easily slip into fear. What will life look like? Will I end up in a wheelchair? Will I need help? Will I be able to see the faces of my loved ones? The opposite of fear is faith. As I remember to put my trust in God, my fears begin to fade. I still may end up in a wheelchair—that has not changed. But my mindset has changed. I am not saying that this is easy or a one-and-done decision. I need to trust God moment by moment. If I end up in a wheelchair, He will be there with me. To "be still and know" is simply being. It is not doing, planning, or worrying. It is resting in God's perfect plan and power. It is being in the present moment. As my friend once told me, "We are human beings, not human doings." (I am not sure who first spoke this quote, but it is accurate nonetheless.) We must stop striving and trying to fix things ourselves. God is in control. Things, people, and situations come and go. Life as we know it will do the same. Nothing on earth is permanent. As my health continues to decline and I lose more function, I want desperately to hold on to what I still have. Instead, I start the grieving process over and over with each new loss. I get frustrated, cry, eat chocolate, and then eventually adjust to my new normal. Then after a while, something else gets worse, and I start the process again. You would think I would be used to it by now, but it catches me off guard every time. When I am so wrapped up in my own suffering and grieving, it is impossible to "be still."

Deep down, I know that this is part of God's plan—not my plan for sure. When we think we know best, we can never be happy. Only God can bring true satisfaction.

While I realize that there are others whose suffering is greater than my own, I am still aware of my glaring, visible, and obvious imperfections, so I mistakenly work hard to make everything else in my life look "perfect." My self-conscious perfectionism only makes me miserable. When we can truly "be still and know" by being present in the moment, all the fears, worries, and imperfections fade away. We can know that we are who and where we are supposed to be. We can have peace even when the world is crashing down around us. God is our refuge, our safe place. We may have to seek that stillness over and over again even within the same day, but it can always be found in the safety of God. People have told me to just sit with God. What does that look like? How do I do that? Simply looking out the window and appreciating the beauty God created helps me to focus on Him. It's not even about bringing my requests to Him. It's about just sitting in silence as if sitting with a close friend. You know, the ones where nothing needs to be said between you, but there is comfort in just being together. This is the same concept.

God loves us just the way we are. We are His creation. He is the one who ordained our imperfections. While God does not create the terrible things of this world, He does allow them to shape us into who He created us to be. "To see through that unsatisfactoriness in a way that can overcome our fear is to hear that cosmic affirmation that we are accepted just as we are…with our limitations and weaknesses. To see and *to accept* those limitations . . . beyond all our idealizations and high expectations, can also enable us to overcome that sense of dissatisfaction."[21]

I, for one, am utterly helpless to change my circumstances. Not only that, but since most of my diseases are advancing, I know there is much more grief to come. The suffering continues. The *only* thing I can do is to "be still and know that [He is] God." I have to completely let go and trust God. All my striving and worrying avails nothing but lost joy. I strongly believe that He gave me this "thorn in the flesh" (2 Cor 12:7) to serve His purposes (more on that in Chapter 6). Life is about God—His will, not mine. The Bible tells us to give thanks in all circumstances (1 Thess 5:18)—not just the good ones, but all. People can grow through suffering, but that does not mean that God sends trials to test us. Instead, it is confirmation that God is in control, and He is with us every step of the way. Every time my health issues progress, He is there. I just need to "be still."

## Setting the Scene

The book of Psalms is a compilation of 150 songs that functioned as the hymnbook of the Old Testament people.[22] The overall ideas in the Psalms acknowledge God's kingship and sovereignty, the behavior and consequences of the righteous and the wicked, God's comfort and protection in times of trouble, the significance of praise

---

[21] Ibid. (emphasis original).
[22] Tremper Longman III, *Introducing the Old Testament* (Grand Rapids, MI: Zondervan, 2012), 92.

in all circumstances, and the function of creation and nature. The psalms are the heart's devoted and inspired reflections on God's divine acts and laws. It is the internalization of the Old Testament. "They have always been, as divinely intended, the model and pattern of acceptable worship, and devotion to God, both privately and publicly. . . . The psalms at times, interpret events in the historical books, furnishing spiritual insights and responses to many situations of life."[23]

Psalm 46 demonstrates that God is with His people in times of distress. It is typically associated with the Assyrian siege of Jerusalem under King Hezekiah in 701 BC. God delivered Hezekiah from the Assyrian king Sennacherib (2 Kings 19) and supernaturally destroyed the Assyrian forces. The psalm was written to reassure God's people that He is their refuge and strength in challenging times. His presence provides comfort.

The core message of Psalm 46 is translated in English as *"Be still and know that I am God."* Another translation interprets the verse like this: "'Desist (from your useless striving and clinging and trying to get the better of the situation), and confess that I am God.' [God basically says,] 'Shut up, I AM in charge here!'"[24] This is the challenge within this psalm.

---

[23] David M. Fleming, and Russell Fuller, "Book of Psalms," in Brand, *Holman Illustrated Bible Dictionary*, 1315.

[24] Habito, *Be Still and Know,* ch. 1.

# Overall Meaning of the Passage

Putting Psalm 46:10 in context with its surrounding verses and chapters helps us to better understand the message. After Psalms 42–44 reveal a supposed absence of God, Psalm 46 focuses on His presence as the protector for His people even though their circumstances may look grim.[25] It encourages readers to appreciate God as the one who intercedes for His people. When read with the preceding psalms, Psalm 46 offers the confidence that God can be trusted. Verses 1–3 describe nature as the shaking mountains and roaring seas rebelling against the people, and verses 4–6 answer these threats with a river representing the presence of God the Creator. Poetically and theologically, the river points to Jerusalem as the city of God, although there is no actual river in Jerusalem. "The holy place where the Most High dwells" (46:4) is the temple that anticipates the eschatological (end-times) kingdom (Rev 22:1). Verse 5 states that the city of God will not be shaken due to God's protection. While the psalm discusses natural disasters, the psalmist also refers to the nations and kingdoms that rebel against Israel and God's will. God wants Israel to stop trying to control their own fate and defense and recognize that He is God, their help and stronghold.

If Psalm 46 is a song, verse 7 is the chorus. It says, "The Lord of hosts is with us; the God of Jacob is our fortress" (ESV). God commands the heavenly armies to protect His people.

---

[25] David G. Firth, "Reading Psalm 46 in Its Canonical Context: An Initial Exploration in Harmonies Consonant and Dissonant," *Bulletin for Biblical Research* 30, no. 1 (2020): 36.

Why is the reference to the "God of Jacob" significant for us? It comes from the passage in Genesis (32:22–32) where Jacob, son of Isaac, son of Abraham, wrestled with God. After wrestling all night, God blessed Jacob and changed his name to Israel which means "he struggles with God." The story symbolizes the struggle for blessing and identity, emphasizing that God is with us in our trials and that perseverance can result in success with a changed fate. "The image of the God of Jacob in Psalm 46 is a guide for us. . . .[t]o wrestle with the God of Jacob . . . We are told: Fear not, trust, and surrender—I AM *an ever-present help in time of distress*."[26] That means we can wrestle with God about things in our lives such as acceptance of our circumstances.

Verses 8–11 join the dangers of natural and moral wickedness together reassuring us that God is powerful and will take care of everything. God essentially yells at His people and commands them to stop struggling and acknowledge Him. The psalm ends with a refrain of the chorus as a reminder to live in God's presence and power,[27] with verse 11 as a song of victory.[28] God is worshiped as a protector for His people.[29] He reigns over natural and moral evil, so His children—not just Israel but every believer—are to trust Him. In other words, "when we say, 'The Lord of Hosts is with us, the God of Jacob is our refuge,' we are asking that God's reign

---

<sup>26</sup> Habito, *Be Still and Know*, ch. 1 (emphasis original).

<sup>27</sup> Rolf A. Jacobson, "Psalm 46: Translation, Structure, and Theology," *Word & World* 40, no. 3 (2020): 318–19.

<sup>28</sup> Theodoret of Cyrus, *Commentary on the Psalms, Psalms 1-72* (Washington, D. C.: Catholic University of America Press, 2000), 272.

<sup>29</sup> Ki-Min Bang, "A Missing Key to Understanding Psalm 46: Revisiting the Chaoskampf," *Conversations with the Biblical World* 37 (2017): 88.

might also happen among us."[30] We are to let Him rule in our hearts and lives.

Following Psalm 46, the focus is the recognition of God as the Most High (Ps 47) and the one who established Zion (which can be used interchangeably with Jerusalem) as the city of God (Ps 48). God is the one to overcome the "stormy" nations, which reminds the people why God is highly exalted.[31]

Psalm 46 is a psalm of trust, and it is also one of strength and comfort, highlighting God's role as a refuge and a source of strength. He has the power to calm the sea and end wars. Verse 10, "Be still, and know that I am God," is a directive to trust in God's power and to acknowledge His sovereignty, even in difficult circumstances. Some scholars say it is His desire that we be still,[32] but it is our choice; meanwhile, others view it as a command. As a command, there is no room for disobedience. It is something we must do. Living in His presence is the most important thing we can do in this life. It brings peace to our hearts and comfort in the worst of times. Psalm 46 shows the love and kindness of God toward His people, especially to those who suffer and struggle against the "roaring sea" (times of trouble). In this verse we see God's total triumph: "No more battle is necessary; God concludes the battle and breaks all the weapons."[33]

---


[30] Jacobson, "Psalm 46," 319–20.

[31] Firth, "Reading Psalm 46 in Its Canonical Context," 37–38.

[32] Mauro-Giuseppe Lepori, "Be Still and Know That I Am God," *The Tablet* 25 (April 2020): 8.

[33] Bang, "A Missing Key to Understanding Psalm 46," 88.

# Discussion of the Verse

Although we live in a different time than the Israelites did, we still suffer and need the encouragement of Psalm 46:10. In this verse, the psalmist shifts from third person to first person, with God as the speaker. When God says to "be still and know," He is giving us His requirements for peace and emphasizing His sovereignty. In order to truly understand, let's break down verse 10 into smaller parts.

**Psalm 46:10:** *"He says, 'Be still, and know that I am God; I will be exalted among the nations, I will be exalted in the earth.'"*

***"Be still."*** This phrase can also be translated as "relax," "let go," or "stop." It entails an act of surrendering control and ceasing striving. It is not necessarily a direct definition in the sense of physically standing still and doing nothing; rather, it reminds us to stop arguing with God and trying to do on our own what only God can do for us. When we rely on our own abilities, we overlook God and forget that He is in control. Knowing that we can trust and submit to His sovereignty creates a calm in our hearts. This requires humility. God reveals His greatness and authority as He delivers His people from bad circumstances, so we are to stop arguing with Him and simply surrender. I say "simply," but it is not actually easy. Do we not believe that God is really in control? May He "help [our] unbelief" (Mark 9:24).

***"And know that I am God."*** The word "know" is typically thought to be knowledge we possess on a particular topic. However, the translation "confess" may give us better insight. This is the acknowledgement that God is God. This emphasizes God's sovereignty and power over all creation. He is perfect, inerrant, and infallible, worthy of sovereignty over everything. As we admit this truth, our way of looking at things changes, then our behavior changes to match our thinking. We surrender our old way of thinking in favor of accepting that God is who He says He is. Then we can allow life to just happen and therefore "be still" with the accompanying peace.[34]

***"'I will be exalted among the nations. I will be exalted in the earth.'"*** Here the nation of Israel is reminded of God's power over all the nations and kingdoms. This tells Israel that in the end, God will be exalted and His sovereignty, power, and glory will be recognized throughout all the world by the righteous and wicked alike, not just His own people. He is "always right and true in everything" He does (Rev 15:3). He has complete victory over all the earth, and everyone should recognize that God's love overcomes evil. We can be confident knowing that God will be exalted. His will and ways will prevail.

# Theological Reflections

"Psalm 46 is theological poetry!"[35] God's protection, presence, and sovereignty are all highlighted in this psalm. God as our "refuge and strength" is the main theological theme in all of the Psalms (Pss 2:12; 16:1; 91:2), and Psalm 46 opens with this same statement of trust in

---

[34] Habito, *Be Still and Know*, ch. 1 (emphasis original).
[35] Jacobson, "Psalm 46," 317.

God as our protector, defender, and sustainer (see also Pss 23; 27; 91), our safe place in times of trouble. He is an active power against disorder and ruin.

God's presence is another theme of Psalm 46. He may not take the suffering away, but He will be present within the difficulty. We are to trust in Him, especially during our trials. The psalm describes natural disasters, but even in the face of these trials, the psalmist asserts, "we will not fear" (46:2) because God is with us. It is our trust in God's presence, not trust in our own ability, that gives us the strength to endure. His presence dwells in the city of God, Jerusalem. Contrary to the roaring sea, the river represents peace and God's presence (46:4). This guarantee of God's presence emphasizes God's protection and refuge.

The other theme of Psalm 46 is God's sovereignty over all creation which is highlighted in verses 8–11. He can end wars and bring peace (46:9). Verse 10 drives home the main message of God's ultimate power. "Be still, and know that I am God" (46:10) is a deep theological proclamation. It invites us to stop striving and to find peace in God's presence and sovereignty. This verse assures us that God is in control. The final verse highlights the opening verse that God is our refuge and strength.

The Book of Psalms anticipates the gospel. Jesus Himself told His disciples that "everything must be fulfilled that is written about me in the Law of Moses, the Prophets and the Psalms" (Luke 24:44 NIV), meaning that the Psalms refer to Him. This is based on the belief that God chose, or elected, David, from whom the King (Messiah, Son) would descend. This is Christ. He is the "the recipient of the worship of the psalms."[36] Jesus came to fulfill the Old Testament, so the entire Old Testament should be viewed through the revelation of God in Jesus.[37]

Psalm 46 tells us that even in the most devastating circumstances, we need not fear because God is in control. "It functions as a declaration to God's people concerning the unimaginable source of strength that is theirs, and ours, in God . . . or . . . in Christ."[38]

Just as God did in Psalm 46, Jesus rebukes the waves, and they obey Him (Matt 8:23–27). The disciples were fretting and panicking in the midst of roaring waters when, once again, all they had to do was be still and look to the One who is in control. This theme repeats when Jesus walks on the water in a stormy sea (Matt 14:24). His disciples feel helpless to get their boat to shore, but Jesus comes to save them from nature as only He can (Matt 14:25). We may not battle literal stormy seas, but, like the disciples, we tend to

---

36 Longman, *Introducing the Old Testament*, 100.
37 Lepori, "Be Still and Know That I Am God," 9.
38 Jacobson, "Psalm 46," 319–20.

lean into our fears instead of trusting Jesus (Matt 14:26). Just as God told Israel to "be still," Jesus tells His followers not to be afraid (Matt 14:27). Once they were able to be still and trust Jesus, the seas calm (Matt 14:32) and they reach the shore (Matt 14:34; John 6:21).[39] This points to Jesus as the One who is exalted as our security and safe place. When we rely on Him, we can "be still" in our circumstances.

# Application

Psalm 46 offers encouragement for us today just as it did for the Israelites so many centuries ago. We have all experienced times when it seems that our lives are falling apart, making it easy to lose sight of God. You may think that this passage is only for those who are experiencing short-term suffering, but for some of us, our actual circumstances will never get better on earth. We will struggle until the day God calls us home, but we can still claim God as our refuge. We do not need to fear. In our daily activities, God invites us to enjoy the peace He promises despite what is happening to us and around us. This is a little piece of being "home." Just like being under that cozy blanket, being in God's presence is where we feel safe and comfortable right now until we can actually go home to heaven.

God does not cause trials so He can play the hero by freeing us from them. No, rather He allows them and then enters into our

---

trials and suffers with us. Jesus underwent agony for us to the extent of dying a criminal's death on the cross. The point of our lives goes well beyond our current trials and whether they are resolved in this life or not. They will be resolved eventually. "The true risk that looms over our life is not the threat of death, but the possibility of living a senseless life, a life that is not stretched toward an ever greater fullness of life, toward a salvation greater even than the restoration of health."[40] God meets us in the middle of our circumstances and walks through them with us. Psalm 46 invites us to pause and remember that God is in control of everything—yes, every single thing. He is stronger than any roaring sea or quaking mountain. He is stronger than a broken marriage, addictions, financial troubles, loss, and health problems. He is stronger than anything we will ever suffer on this earth. We need not fight for ourselves. We only need to "be still and know that [He] is God."

But how do we put this into practice? Being still can involve prayer. Praying the Bible verses about trusting God in difficult times is one way we can depend on God. To pray, we must be still and silent. "Silence is not merely negative—a pause between words, a temporary cessation of speech—but, properly understood, it is highly positive: an attitude of attentive alertness, a vigilance, and above all of listening."[41] It is a calm, meditative state of mind. "Silence is a privileged entry into the realm of God and into eternal life . . . for silence is a language that is infinitely deeper, more far reaching,

---

[40] Ibid., 9.

[41] Archimandrite Kallistos Ware, "Be Still, and Know That I Am God (Psalm 46:10)," *Parabola* 33, no 1 (2008): 68.

more understanding, more compassionate, and more eternal than any other language. . . . There is nothing in the world that resembles God as much as silence."[42]

When we study the historical background, literary structure, and theological themes, we can understand Psalm 46:10 in a deeper way and see its relevance for our own lives. It reminds us to trust God and His unchanging character in the midst of whatever we are going through. We place our hope in Him. "The Lord Almighty is with us" (Ps 46:11). We can be sure that God will be faithful to us. One day there will be no more suffering (Rev 21:4). This is not just wishful thinking. It is a promise. We can look forward to living in God's presence and promises for eternity. As God commands us to "be still," we are to acknowledge that He alone is God; therefore, we need not fear anything. He is our help, strength, confidence, security, and shelter. He is greater than anything life can throw at us. Being still is a reminder to stop trying to handle things that are not mine to control. I know that one day I will be in God's kingdom dancing like I used to before my health deteriorated. Until then, I will "be still."

---

[42] Meister Eckhart, "Be Still, and Know That I Am God (Psalm 46:10)," *Parabola* 33, no 1 (2008): 71.

### *Literary and Historical Context*

"The Hebrew title of the book means 'praises.' The English title (Psalms) comes from the Septuagint, the ancient Greek translation of the Hebrew Old Testament. The Greek word *psalmoi* means 'songs,' from which comes the idea, 'songs of praises' or 'praise songs.'"[43]

The book of Psalms is divided into five sections generally grouped by type—praise, lament, prayer, thanksgiving, and hymn. Additionally, there are psalms of remembrance, confidence, wisdom, kingship, and trust. Psalm 46 is a psalm of trust. "Do not fear" is a common characteristic of the psalms of trust. In Psalm 46, confidence comes from knowing that God is protecting His people from terrible danger. The first verse of Psalm 46 declares trust and confidence in God: "God is our refuge and strength, an ever-present help in trouble" (Ps 46:1 NIV), even in the midst of natural disasters (mountains falling into the sea, roaring seas, and earthquakes). If God can overcome natural disasters, He can be trusted in everything.

Each individual psalm contributes to the overall message of the Book of Psalms. They are not just literary works—poems, songs, and hymns—but they maintain historical accuracy as well.[44]

---

[43] Fleming and Fuller, "Book of Psalms," 1313.
[44] Firth, "Reading Psalm 46 in Its Canonical Context," 23.

**Author:** Authorship within the Psalms is typically identified in the title of each Psalm. For Psalm 46, authorship is credited to the Sons of Korah. This was one of the most well-known groups of temple singers (2 Chr 20:19). Many of their psalms may be from their handbook.[45] The book of Psalms as we know it did not come together until after the exile, so the editor(s) who organized the psalms should be distinguished from the authors who wrote the individual psalms.[46]

**Date:** These individual psalms cover a one-thousand-year period from the time of Moses (fifteenth century BC) to after the exile (fifth century BC).

**Historical Time and Background:** Psalm 46 was written during a time of conflict. Tradition dictates some general assumptions in understanding Psalm 46. It was well-known that God lived in His city (Jerusalem) and that both He and His people were under attack. God reveals Himself through His actions in times of war as well as peace. God always wins—no weapon formed against His people can prosper (Isa 54:17)—therefore, God's people do not need to fight for control. The situation here is that the city of God was being attacked by multiple nations. God's people were "still"—they recognized God's sovereignty and power, so they stopped striving and surrendered their control of the situation to God. God stepped in and destroyed the weapons of the nations, then God's people sang on behalf of their city.

---

[45] Mike Mitchell and Phil Logan, "Korah," in Brand, *Holman Illustrated Bible Dictionary*, 979.

[46] Hill and Walton, *A Survey of the Old Testament*, 420.

**Geographic Context:** Psalm 46 is not explicit in its details regarding the name of "the city of God, the holy place where the Most High dwells" (Ps 46:4) or its geographical location (although Jerusalem is assumed); however, it mentions mountains, sea, and a river with streams, which would imply a northern setting such as the city of Dan. Since the city is near major rivers, floods were common, so the ancient people saw the stormy waters as evil. This location also experienced strong earthquakes due to the city's location on a fault line. The battle theme originates from the idea that natural catastrophes disrupt the systems that God created. God does not intend to remove the threats; rather, God protects humanity and the ecosystem from the threats of the unseen powers behind natural disasters. The first step towards an ecological understanding of Psalm 46 is to see God as the defender of the planet rather than its destroyer.[47] Psalm 46 is divided into three sections, with each one describing a different earthquake around 750 BC and showing God as protecting His people from the earthquake.[48] The original audience would have understood this since they were living in the days of these intense earthquakes.

**Literary Background:** Mesopotamian and Egyptian hymns and prayers offer context that help us appreciate the psalms. Although these differ from the Israelite psalms, examining their form and content helps with analysis. The psalms are arranged into three

---

[47] Bang, "A Missing Key to Understanding Psalm 46," 78–80.

[48] Ibid., 85–86.

main categories—praise, lament, and wisdom—each with a mostly reliable arrangement, and each easily identifiable.[49] Whereas the Mesopotamians tend to combine praise and lament, the Israelites praise God's attributes rather than only asking for answers to prayer. Most notably, Mesopotamian laments include incantations and magical ceremonies to force the deity into compliance with their request. The worshiper assumes the guilt without any knowledge of what the deity finds offensive; therefore, more of a cultic ritual is fulfilled to please the god. In the laments of the Israelites, however, the people generally consider themselves to be blameless and therefore look for exoneration without any incantations or magic. While the content may be similar in that they are both laments, there is a theological difference relating to the conflicting views of God and how He should be worshiped.[50]

**Structure and Organization:** Psalms are arranged like music written for worship services to meditate on God's character and the individual's response.[51] Psalms are grouped according to the psalmist like David or the Sons of Korah. While the reasoning behind the order of the psalms is not obvious, it is noteworthy that most of the earlier psalms focus on lament that turn into hymns as the book progresses. By its form, the book of Psalms shows how God can turn "weeping into dancing" (Ps 30:11).[52]

---

[49] Hill and Walton, *A Survey of the Old Testament*, 423.
[50] Ibid., 425–26.
[51] Ibid., 428–29.
[52] Longman, *Introducing the Old Testament*, 93.

**Genre and Literary Style:** The book of Psalms is classified as poetry, with some of these poems meant to be sung, such as Psalm 46; therefore, they can also be classified as songs.[53]

**Biblical Context:** The Psalms are authoritative as Scripture. Second Timothy 3:16 says, "All Scripture is God-breathed and is useful for teaching, rebuking, correcting and training in righteousness" (NIV). Psalm 46 shows trust in God as refuge who can overcome any situation, a common theme throughout the entire Bible. The position of Psalm 46 within the Book of Psalms enhances our reading of it in its canonical context as it exalts God and expresses why humanity need not fear.[54]

**Approaches to Interpretation of Psalm 46:**

There are five different approaches to interpreting Psalm 46 as detailed below:

*Messianic Approach.* In the classical and neoclassical commentaries, the psalm is seen as prophetic, pointing to the final redemption. It is believed that the authors, the Sons of Korah, are the same Sons of Korah who rebelled against Moses yet survived the consequences of their rebellion. They then understood that Israel would survive their ordeal. The river may be one of those flowing from the garden of Eden in the city of God, Jerusalem, whereas others say the city of God comprises the entire land of Isreal. The psalm may also refer to the messianic context of Gog and Magog, a battle against Israel that comes before the return of

---

[53] Ibid., 97.
[54] Firth, "Reading Psalm 46 in Its Canonical Context," 39.

Jesus, as described in the books of Ezekiel and Revelation, with the earthquakes representing the wars to come before the messianic era. The end of the psalm can be seen as a prophecy about the wars that will ring in the messianic era.[55]

*Historical Approach.* This view sees the psalm as historical, reflecting thanksgiving after Jerusalem was saved from the Assyrian army during Hezekiah's reign in Judah. The Assyrian king demanded the surrender of Jerusalem, ridiculing King Hezekiah's trust in God. Hezekiah responded by praying for deliverance. God heard his prayer and sent an angel to strike down a multitude of Assyrian soldiers, causing their withdrawal (2 Kings 19) and displaying God's faithfulness and sovereignty in a difficult circumstance. The river may be the Gihon that accumulates at the base of ancient Jerusalem, which was also highlighted in the Judeo-Assyrian conflict. This confirms the geographical context of the psalm and chronology in ancient Jerusalem.[56]

*Metaphorical Approach.* This analysis reminds Israel that devotion to God will result in His protection and prosperity. This message should be shared with the world, uniting humanity, resulting in the worship of one God. Trials, wars, and disasters are all events through which God's goodness is to be understood. This view holds that the earthquake and raging seas is a metaphor for trials, with God as Israel's strength and confidence during

---

[55] Arie Folger, "Understanding Psalm 46," *Jewish Bible Quarterly* 41, no. 1 (2013): 38.

[56] Ibid., 39.

inevitable suffering. God will not allow His people to fall.[57]

*Synthesis Approach.* This interpretation claims that the psalm is prophetic and that the disasters in it are retributions and reprimands. The theme of natural disasters and devastation of Israel's opponents are often joined in the Bible (Isa 17:12; Ezek 38:20; 39:3–9; Joel 4:16; Zech 14:6–8; Judg. 5:4; Mic 1:3–4; Nah 1:1–6). In this approach, Psalm 46 is a psalm of prophecy of Isaiah, Ezekiel, Joel, and Zecheriah, therefore representing the historical past and future redemption.[58]

*Simple Reading.* In this interpretation, the psalmist shows confidence and trust in God when confronted with impending trials. This belief comes from knowing that God is in Jerusalem protecting His City; however, postexilic Jerusalem did fall. This can be resolved by considering the psalm is not referring to ancient Jerusalem but rather to end-of-days Jerusalem. The messianic era is when Jerusalem will be under God's protection. Although Jerusalem has been destroyed repeatedly, God's people continue to survive.

While there is no one interpretation that trumps the others, most interpretations agree that Psalm 46 is associated with the coming of the messianic era with the goal of encouraging confidence that Isreal will triumph.[59]

---

[57] Ibid., 39–40.
[58] Ibid., 41.
[59] Ibid., 41–42.

Chapter 4

# WHAT IS THE PURPOSE OF TRIALS?

## James 1:2–4

*"Consider it pure joy, my brothers and sisters, whenever you face trials of many kinds, because you know that the testing of your faith produces perseverance. Let perseverance finish its work so that you may be mature and complete, not lacking anything."* (NIV)

Yippee! Trials and suffering! Again. More. Worse. On the surface, this does not sound like something joyful. I am not out buying a cake to celebrate each time my health worsens and I lose more function. So what does this passage really mean? Why would James want us to consider suffering "pure joy"? Sometimes I feel like I literally cannot take one more step. I cannot manage one more progression, one more loss, or one more trial. I am not feeling joyful! I convince myself that I am holding it together and managing my diseases, then I stub my toe and burst into tears.

When I went in for an annual checkup last year, the doctor diagnosed me with an entirely new, unrelated disease. I told him that was not how I thought this appointment was going to go. The doctor asked me what I was expecting, and I responded with, "How about:

'Nice to see you. See you next year!'?" We both laughed as he told me that he doesn't want to sit near me because I have a dark cloud hanging over me with such an unfortunate concoction of multiple unrelated diseases. Yikes! Just what you want to hear from your doctor. After laughing it off in his office, I went home and thought about it. One more disease? Really? Why does it not end? God must think I am abnormally strong to handle so much.

All the progression and diagnoses are more than just a physical journey. The emotional path is almost worse than progressing health complications. Do I cry? More often than I would like to admit. But I also cry out to God. It is my faith that allows me to get up and move forward. Remembering that this life is temporary brings peace to my heart. I must endure. I realize that when I persevere, my faith becomes stronger. God must be developing me for something amazing in heaven. Sometimes I really wonder what that could be, but I trust His plan. That does not mean that it is easy or that I can dismiss my own feelings in exchange for His purposes. I can be sad, angry, or whatever the feeling of the day may be, and I can also trust that He knows best and that there is purpose in the pain. The challenge for us is to focus on the eternal, not the temporary. Sure, no problem. (Insert "smack my head" emoji here.) Do I wish God would take all these diseases from me or at least stop them from progressing? Of course I do! But the truth is that these trials are developing my faith in God. Having faith is easy when things are going well. It is in the suffering where our belief is tested. Without confidence in Jesus and the eternal life He provides, this life is the only one we get, which would mean that the suffering will actually never end. That is a scary thought. It is through our faith while suffering that we learn how to endure. Our perseverance matures our faith. Are we supposed to be excited about suffering? Should we look for opportunities to suffer so that we grow? No, but as we rejoice in our difficult circumstances, we are living examples of our trust in God. He will, without a doubt, use our suffering for our good and His glory. This passage assures us that there are purposes and benefits that accompany enduring trials. The result is patience, perseverance, maturity, resoluteness, and godliness. James asks us to look at trials from a different perspective than just pain and suffering. Rather than allowing our circumstances to drown us in despair, we can find joy in knowing that God is walking through it with us (Ps 23:4; Isa 43:2; Heb 13:5) and growing us into godly people as He intended.

The Message phrases James 1:2–4 this way: "Consider it a sheer gift, friends, when tests and challenges come at you from all sides. You know that under pressure, your faith-life is forced into the open and shows its true colors. So don't try to get out of anything prematurely. Let it do its work so you become mature and well-developed, not deficient in any way." Not only arc trials to be considered joy, but they are also in fact a "gift." Really? Did it come with a return receipt? I would like to exchange it for smooth sailing and good circumstances, please. I would like to return these leg braces and limp in exchange for high heels and the ability to dance again. Clearly James is referring to a different type of joy, one that has nothing to do with our situation. He is referring to the joy that keeps us calm as our world is falling apart. It is the peace that comes from knowing God is with us. He will refine us through challenging times, and we will be made stronger and more Christ-like. That is the gift. It reminds me of that old saying, "That which does not kill us makes us stronger."

The opposite of perseverance is indifference. The opposite of faith is fear. The opposite of joy is sadness. We are going to go through trials and suffer no matter our attitude. The way I see it, we have two choices. We can focus on being fearful and sad during our troubles, or we can persevere, trust God, and be joyful knowing that we are in the midst of God's will. The choice is ours.

## Setting the Scene

James is typically thought of as a book that emphasizes the importance of works, but works are important because they are vital to true faith. In fact, it is our faith that makes us want to do the good works. What are these good works? They are acts of kindness, love, compassion, and serving others, to name a few. These works are the result of true faith that display a changed heart. For example, before I came to know Jesus, my concern was usually selfish. I wanted to make sure that if I did something good, there was something in it for me. Now, I do good works, not with the hope of recognition but rather because of my love for God. It is faith in action. James encourages his readers to see trials from an eternal perspective. He emphasizes that true faith can be seen in the way a believer speaks and acts in the world. The main themes in the book are to love the wisdom of Jesus, to reflect real faith through actions, and to be patient and persevere in difficulties.

Through his own experiences, James knew firsthand that trials are gifts that result in endurance and molding our character so we may be "perfect and complete" (1:4). James uses the word "perfect" repeatedly throughout his book (1:4; 17, 25; 2:8, 23; 3:2). This theme of perfection or wholehearted devotion to God is the translation for the original word *teleios*.[60] It typically means "perfect," but a more accurate definition would be complete, whole, spiritually mature, lacking nothing, or having achieved its purpose. *Telios* is achieved through steadfastness in trials which is a process, not a one-time event. This word refers to the wholeness of living out one's belief in Jesus. This is much different from being a perfect and sinless person. As we know, not one of us can ever be perfect on this side of heaven. Rather, this perfection is achieved through viewing suffering from God's perspective (1:5–8), seeking His wisdom, and trusting that He is more powerful than our circumstances. Ultimate perfection is being conformed to the image of Jesus. James highlights the idea that perfection in the Christian life is seen through right living, not actual perfection. Right living includes accepting our trials and suffering as part of God's plan. This can be difficult, so we are to ask God for the wisdom to live right (1:5) without any doubt that God can answer. If we ask without faith, the Bible says we should not expect to receive this wisdom (1:7–8), so our faith is crucial to our "perfection" in achieving godliness.

James leads his audience through a seven-step process toward

---

[60] Darian R. Lockett, *Letters for the Church: Reading James, 1–2 Peter, 1–3 John, and Jude as Canon,* (Westmont: InterVarsity Press, 2021), 30–31.

godliness: "(1) confront trials (1:2–18), (2) please God (1:19–27), (3) demonstrate faith (2:1–26), (4) control self (3:1–18), (5) set priorities (4:1–10), (6) live for eternity (4:12–5:6), and (7) trust God (5:7–18)."[61] James focuses on endurance through suffering much like the messages of the apostles Paul (Rom 5:3–4) and Peter (1 Pet 1:6–7).

# Overall Meaning of the Passage

James is concerned with the faith of his audience. He stresses that a person's attitude and actions must align with faith. "James writes his letter in response to the sufferings, trials, and temptations that threatened the integrity of the community of those who believed in Jesus as Lord and Christ. . . . James reminds the audience that trials are part of the package of faith and yield good fruit at the end of the day."[62] Hardships can leave us confused, but joy in adversity comes from knowing God, and that wisdom enables us to handle life's struggles.

James 1:2–4 is viewed as a syllogism (deductive reasoning), saying that "'the believer who experiences trials must be happy.' The proof of the argument runs as follows:

- If there are trials, then there is testing (= refining) of faith.
- If there is testing (= refining) of faith, then there is endurance in faith.
- If there is endurance in faith, then there must be perfect works.
- If there are perfect works, then a perfect character develops.

---

[61] Eric Brandell, "Discerning the Literary Structure in the Epistle of James," *Stone-Campbell Journal* 25, no. 2 (2022): 237.

[62] Dan G. McCartney, Robert Yarbrough, and Robert Stein, *James* (Grand Rapids, MI: Baker Academic, 2009), 81.

- If there is a perfect character, then each virtue is possessed and each fully developed.
- If each virtue is possessed and each fully developed, then the believer will receive the crown of life.
- If the believer is to receive the crown of life, he will be happy."[63]

The premise is that some action, difficult situation, or adversity must be endured in order to gain eternal life. Here, the specific situation is not named. Endurance in faith could be translated as genuineness (good heart), testing (self-control), means of testing faith (persistence) (Luke 8:15, 2 Pet 1:6, and Rev 2:19), good works (Rom 2:7), or against adversity (2 Cor 1:6), leaving nine possible interpretations:

(1) The genuineness of your faith results in endurance in faith.
(2) The genuineness of your faith results in endurance in good works.
(3) The genuineness of your faith results in endurance against adversity.
(4) The testing of your faith results in endurance in faith.
(5) The testing of your faith results in endurance in good works.
(6) The testing of your faith results in endurance against adversity.
(7) The means of testing your faith results in endurance in faith.
(8) The means of testing your faith results in endurance in good works.
(9) The means of testing your faith results in endurance against adversity.[64]

Most options can be eliminated since they do not fit the context. The possibilities in (7) to (9) allude to a procedure (the way faith is

---

[63] J. L. P. Wolmarans, "Making Sense out of Suffering: James 1:2–4," *HTS Teologiese Studies / Theological Studies* 47, no. 4 (1991): 1109.

[64] Ibid., 1112.

tested) rather than actual faith. Options (1) to (3) refer to the quality of an action or object (genuineness) which is not something in and of itself that proves genuine faith. This leaves (4) to (6) as the only viable translations.[65]

Refining faith is much like refining metal, and here, James indirectly compares the two (James 1:3–4). The process of testing or refining metal eliminates impurities, resulting in the rest of the metal becoming strong. This parallels with human testing and refining through suffering.[66] It is the trials that refine our faith so we can become strong just like refined metal. Our attitude toward adversity reflects our faith. Circumstances may be out of our control, but we can manage our response through wisdom and a faithful outlook of joy because trials "are an opportunity to endure and prove faith-keeping. . . . because they lead to wisdom. This is not to say that there is no component of sorrow in trials as well. . . . The reason for the joy is not the suffering per se, but rather its fruit, the character traits that it induces: endurance, maturity, and wisdom. The strange ability to experience joy at the same time as sorrow is a hallmark of genuine faith."[67] Joy and wisdom include discipline and testing. Ugh. That is never what we want to hear, but when we can suffer well knowing that Jesus's return is imminent, that is when we find joy and become strong like refined metal without the impurities.

How long must we endure? James often uses the terms "trials" and "endurance" in an eschatological (concerned with the

---

[65] Ibid., 1113.
[66] Ibid., 1113.
[67] McCartney, Yarbrough, and Stein, *James*, 84.

final events in the history of the world and destiny of humankind)
context just as Peter and Paul do (1 Pet 1:7; Rom 5:3–4). He relates
overcoming trials with receiving the "crown of life" (1:12), another
reference to eternal life. This suggests that James's "perfection" has
the future in mind; however, he makes it clear that this perfection
should begin developing now with a heart that is fully devoted to
God.[68] Therefore, endurance must last until Christ's return or as long
as the testing remains. This would mean that "perfection"
(wholeness, completeness) at the coming of Christ will result in the
reward of receiving the crown of life (1:12). From this premise, joy
lives in the expectation of Christ's return, at which time things will
be overturned—those who are sad will become joyful. In the
meantime, joy comes from doing good works during trials.[69] So
while I am limping around and leaning on my service dog, I can still
smile and be friendly. I can still give a listening ear to a struggling
friend. I can still support my husband. We may not always be able to
make sense of our suffering, but we should not give in to our
worries, fears, and anger. If we leave faith out of the equation, the
result is hopelessness.

---

[68] Lockett, *Letters for the Church*, 31.
[69] Wolmarans, "Making Sense out of Suffering," 118–19.

# Discussion of Individual Verses

Before we jump into the individual verses, let's take a look at the
New Testament scholar Blomberg's summary of James 1:2–4:

> The initial treatment of trials causes believers to view them as
> opportunities for rejoicing (v. 2a). The two subordinate
> adverbial clauses define the time and basis for this command.
> Not just in some situations but "whenever" trials beset a
> person (v. 2b), one must rejoice, because the circumstances
> can build character—in this case, most notably by fostering
> perseverance (v. 3a). The second imperative follows from the
> specific ethical observation: believers must allow
> perseverance to mold them into what God wants (v. 4a). The
> purpose for this command is stated positively and then
> restated negatively. As Christians grow, they come closer and
> closer to maturity or wholeness, that is, to a state in which
> they no longer remain significantly spiritually deficient (v.
> 4bc).[70]

Blomberg is saying that according to James, Christians should
rejoice in trials because they develop character by cultivating
perseverance which then leads believers toward spiritual maturity.

**James 1:2** *"Consider [count] it pure joy, my brothers and sisters,
whenever you face trials of many kinds."*

**"Consider."** This requires thought, as in weighing the facts of our
situation. Alternately, "count" is used instead of "consider" in some
versions. To "count" is to add up all the data to reach a conclusion. It
has nothing to do with emotion. So, we are to think about our trials

---

[70] Craig L. Blomberg, and Mariam J. Kovalishyn, *James* (Grand Rapids, MI: Zondervan Academic, 2008), ch. 1.

as "pure joy" whether we feel that way or not.

*"Pure."* Something that is free from contamination is considered to be pure. Here, it means to have a heart completely devoted to God, free from conflicting loyalties.

*"Joy."* James declares trials as reasons for joy. He does not tell us to resign ourselves to trials, rather we are to be joyful. Joy is the correct response to times of testing. Joy refers to "a state of being rather than an emotion. Joy proves quite different from happiness, so this verse does *not* support the idea that a Christian must smile all the time! Joy may be defined as a settled contentment in every situation or 'an unnatural reaction of deep, steady and unadulterated thankful trust in God.'"[71] "Counting it all joy" is faith's response to trials, knowing that we are becoming spiritually mature.

*"Brothers and sisters."* These are James's fellow believers in Christ, specifically the Diaspora messianic Jews (the Jews who were scattered outside the land of ancient Israel). In the Old Testament, it means fellow Israelites (Lev 25:46; Deut 15:3), and in the New Testament it refers to fellow Christians (Acts 2:29; 3:17). The church is God's people who call Him Father, making them children of God. This would make all the children siblings;[72] therefore, the term "brothers and sisters" denotes equality with James.

*"Whenever."* James does not tell us to look for trouble, but when we find ourselves in trials, we are to look at it as a good thing. Just because we are Christians does not mean that we will not face hardships. James said "when," not "if," we face trials.

---

[71] Ibid. (emphasis original).
[72] McCartney, Yarbrough, and Stein, *James*, 93.

***"You face trials of many kinds."*** Life is full of trials—many, recuring, new ones, different ones. We aren't given only one trial in life, instead we are tested repeatedly. There are two types of testing—voluntary that causes sinful pleasure, temptations from the devil, or pride—the things that tempt us to stray from God; and involuntary trials that afflict our bodies, including things like poverty and health issues. James is saying that if one experiences involuntary trials, then joy should be experienced as well.[73] James is referring to trials that would bring the truth of God's sovereignty into question, so he wants us to stay strong in our faith when we are being tested by trials and suffering. This is the proof of true faith. "Trials" are expected, so we are to be prepared. This is how we serve the Lord. We are to view trials as the way to blessings and reward (1:12). These are not only daily trials, but these can be life-altering, never-ending trials.

When read all together, James 1:2 presents joy as the remedy to suffering. This is not a call to be brave in the face of trials; rather, it is a command to view suffering as joy. How do we do this when it is contrary to what we feel? When we understand that we can delight in our suffering, we can celebrate our growth and the certainty that we will be rewarded (1:12). James wants us to know that our trials and temptations are reasons to praise God because when we endure them for His sake, they increase our love for God. It sounds counterintuitive, but trials grow us to maturity. If we run from our trials (if that were even possible), we are running from the reward of

---

[73] Wolmarans, "Making Sense out of Suffering," 1112.

eternal life too; therefore, these trials are for our ultimate benefit.[74]

**James 1:3** *"Because you know that the testing of your faith produces perseverance."*

**"Because."** This is the why. Why should we consider trials joy? James is going to tell us.

**"You know."** We already know that trials sharpen us, and the people who James was writing to would have known this too. This knowledge comes from biblical teaching that says testing will develop godly character if we are faithful, including Old Testament teaching and Jesus's words. This theme can be seen throughout the New Testament (Rom 5:1–5; 1 Pet 1:6–9; Heb 12:11; 2 Cor 1:8–9).

**"Testing of your faith."** The trials in life create the opportunity to prove the genuineness of our faith in God. This testing is meant to refine our faith, not to break us down. This in turn produces perseverance and steadfastness that lead to spiritual maturity. The point is that we are to view hardships as opportunities to build endurance and deepen our relationship with God. The testing of faith produces endurance as a way of recognizing testing as joy. Trials reveal our level of faith to ourselves and to others. True faith is found in surrender. Our faith determines our salvation. Faith comes from hearing (Rom 10:17), knowing, and obeying the Word of God. God allows these trials in order to prove our faith. Our faith proves that we are God's children.

The involuntary testing—the things that cause suffering as

---

[74] Saint Nicodemus of the Holy Mountain, "Explanation of the Epistle of St. James," trans. Hieromonk (Papa) Ephraim, *The Orthodox Word* 58, no. 3 (2022): 122–23.

opposed to temptations—are the ones we are to count as joy. Second Corinthians 4:16–18 says, "Therefore we do not lose heart. Though outwardly we are wasting away, yet inwardly we are being renewed day by day. For our light and momentary troubles are achieving for us an eternal glory that far outweighs them all. So we fix our eyes not on what is seen, but on what is unseen, since what is seen is temporary, but what is unseen is eternal" (NIV).

*"Perseverance."* This is also called steadfastness. It is an active determination, not a passive waiting which means that we are to hold onto the truth regardless of circumstances. It is choosing to stay in a difficult situation instead of trying to avoid it. Just as metal is tested by fire for its strength, our faith is tested in trials, and the beauty is displayed for all to see. It is staying the course without giving up, even in an unpleasant, painful, or difficult situation. We cling to the hope of Jesus's return when we will no longer endure suffering.

**James 1:4** *"Let perseverance finish its work so that you may be mature and complete, not lacking anything."*

*"Let perseverance finish its work."* James commands Christians to work at perfection, and he tells us how. In order to persevere, we must tolerate all trials. Our perseverance must outweigh our suffering. James is commanding us to submit to the will of God. Perseverance requires patience which builds character "so that someone who possesses it cannot be overcome. . . . Trials demonstrate the purity of faith, which is made perfect by the patient

endurance of affliction."[75]

***"So that you may be mature and complete."*** The finished work is achieving spiritual maturity (Eph 4:13–16). Through perseverance we will become whole; therefore, trials have a good purpose. James reminds us not to be impatient in favor of comfort but rather to endure for a lasting reward.

Although we are called to be mature and complete (Matt 5:48; 1 Cor 14:20; Phil 3:15; Col 4:12; 1 Pet 1:16), we know that we can never be perfect, or complete, here on earth, but we will reach perfection when Jesus returns. The best we can do on this side of heaven is to aim for maturity which is achieved through endurance. James's entire message is that of being "mature," "perfect," or "full-grown," translated from the key word "*teleios*. . . . The word *perfect* entails wholehearted or single-minded devotion to God. Maturity is becoming who God intended us to be, a "perfected" human in the image of Jesus. James contrasts maturity (perfection) and completeness with the man of an uncertain, or divided, mind (1:6–8). Combining "perfect" with the word "complete" suggests sacrifice. If sacrifice is an offering to God, I am offering the comfort of good health, the ability to walk well, and all the other details in exchange for maturity in Jesus. What is your sacrifice? Can you offer it to God knowing that you will be complete one day?

In the Old Testament, when a lamb was sacrificed for atonement, it had to be perfect, without blemish (Exod 12:5). In keeping with that requirement, Jesus was the perfect lamb who was

---

[75] Gerald L. Bray, and Thomas C. Oden, eds. *James, 1-2 Peter, 1-3 John, Jude* (Westmont: InterVarsity Press, 2000), 74–75.

sacrificed for our sins (Heb 9:11–4). James is saying that we also must be perfect (mature and complete) without flaws. When we choose to sacrifice our version of "perfect" (smart, beautiful, successful, etc.) and endure our trials here on earth, we will become whole in the eyes of God. "The meaning is clear: the strengthening of endurance through trials is an important aspect of Christian life, and without it, the Christian is ill-equipped for service to God,"[76] which is our greatest purpose.

***"Not lacking anything."*** We have everything we need, and we do not miss the mark. It means we are fully equipped for eternity. Testing of faith can result in steadfastness that, when mature, enables us to be perfect, complete, and lacking in nothing.[77]

# Theological Reflections

James's theological approach teaches about creation, God's goodness, the God-like characteristics of humanity, divine judgment, loyalty to God, following Jesus's example of love, loving others regardless of their socioeconomic status, and faith regardless of circumstances. He also warns against being undecided or half-hearted; James is concerned with his audience loving God with everything they have—heart, soul, and strength (Deut 6:5). James's theology is in keeping with the rest of the Bible. His teaching is based on the ethical teachings of the Old Testament and Jewish

---

[76] McCartney, Yarbrough, and Stein, *James*, 87–88.

[77] Paige Patterson, "Letter from James," in Brand, *Holman Illustrated Bible Dictionary*, 853.

wisdom, as well as the teachings of Jesus, especially the Sermon on the Mount (Matt 5–7) which includes the message of selflessness, compassion, and love. Paul's doctrine teaches salvation through faith alone, whereas James teaches that genuine faith produces good works. Everything James says supports the fact that his God is the unchanging, righteous, gracious, forgiving God of Israel.[78] Creation and eschatology are evident in James's writing. James utilizes the initial chapters of Genesis to characterize God, to explain his understanding of humanity, and to establish his call for ethical behavior.[79]

James applies his theology to reinforce the likely positive outcome of trials. Difficult circumstances are an occasion to build character. Verses 2–4 are not an automatic promise. Suffering doesn't *guarantee* maturity. Rather than repeat the rebellion of the Israelites wandering in the desert (Numbers), James's audience can do it differently by finding joy in their suffering. If the Israelites had stopped rebelling against God during their wandering, they would have arrived in the promised land much sooner. It was only a forty-day trip, but their rebellion kept them wandering for forty years. Similar to James 1:4, Romans 5:2–5 and 1 Peter 1:6–7 also describe the necessity of rejoicing in various trials and suffering because it will develop authentic faith. James, Paul, and Peter most likely all based their advice on early Christian ethical custom. Rejoicing in difficulties is not easy, especially when there is no end in sight;

---

[78] Dale C. Allison Jr., *James: A Critical and Exegetical Commentary*, International Critical Commentary (London: Bloomsbury, 2013), 89.

[79] Joel B. Green, "Betwixt and Between: The Letter of James and the Human Condition," The Biblical Annals 12, no. 2 (December 31, 2022), 300.

however, finding joy develops maturity. This is not faking it so others think we are fine. (I have to admit that I do this sometimes simply so people don't feel sorry for me.) We cannot wish our way into joy rather than depression, but we can "consider" and "know" that God works everything for our good and His purposes (Rom 8:28) when we allow Him to work through every circumstance in our lives. Although we may not understand why we must suffer, we know that "our light and momentary troubles are achieving for us an eternal glory that far outweighs them all" (2 Cor 4:17). Rather than referring to an emotion, James is referring to "a theological perception of trials, which considers their complete demise by God who promises a new day."[80] Stated plainly, it means that when Jesus returns, there will be no more suffering (Rev 21:4; Rom 8:18; John 3:16; 2 Pet 3:13). Hallelujah!

# Pointing to Jesus

The book of James is more theocentric (God-centered) than Christocentric (Christ-centered), lacking much information about Christ; however, there are some similarities between the teachings of Jesus and James. Since James's current audience is already anticipating Christ's return (5:6–8), they understand the incorporation of Jesus's teachings from His Sermon on the Mount (Matt 5–7), including such topics as: "spiritual poverty" (Matt 5:3; Jas 1:9); "meekness" (Matt 5:5, 7; Jas 1:21); "peacemakers" (Matt

---

[80] Blomberg and Kovalishyn, *James*, ch. 1.

5:9; Jas 3:18); the risk of "taking oaths" (Matt 5:34–37; Jas 5:12); "deception of riches" (Matt 6:19; Jas 5:2); and that "a tree is known by its fruit" (Matt 7:16; Jas 3:12). James also shows influence from the wisdom book of Proverbs (Prov 1–9). James teaches how to follow Jesus in the midst of the problems of this world.[81] The end times is expected and assumed in James, so Christ is assumed. James declares that the Lord "will return" (5:7–9); there will be a final judgment (2:12–13; 3:1; 4:12; 5:9); that judgment is near (5:7–9); and it will mean salvation (eschatological reward) for the righteous (1:12, 21; 2:5; 4:10; 5:20) and retribution for others (2:13; 3:6; 5:3).[82] James asserts that the hope of being rewarded when Jesus returns is what encourages us to persevere.

# Application

It is not easy to endure suffering patiently. Trust me, I know! Sometimes it literally feels like my feet are in concrete, and I cannot move forward. We must endure life's trials through perseverance, godly wisdom, and prayer. James lets his readers "know that the trials they are enduring will test their faith, but that the outcome of the process will be perseverance (1:2–4). . . .[T]hey can persevere because they know that the Lord is coming and is near. . . . James does not teach them simply to be passive, but to be determined in faith with tenacity, joy, and true grit."[83] This sounds good on paper,

---

[81] Gary M. Burge, and Gene L. Green, *The New Testament in Antiquity,* 2nd ed. (Grand Rapids, MI: Zondervan Academic, 2020), 500.

[82] Allison, *James,* 92.

[83] Burge and Green, *The New Testament in Antiquity,* 506–7.

but how do we actually do this?

There are practical ways to experience joy and maturity during trials. We can start to look at suffering differently—as a blessing, not a curse. We can (and should) practice gratitude, pray, depend on God's strength, and serve others to get our minds off of ourselves. By the renewing of our minds (Rom 12:2), we can transform our perspective on suffering. Being in God's Word is the best way to align our thinking with His. Through life in Christ and the indwelling of the Holy Spirit, strengthened by wisdom, our thoughts and attitudes can be characterized by joy instead of misery. God tells us to give thanks in all circumstances (1 Thess 5:18), and gratitude shifts our attention away from our suffering. The spiritual habits of Bible reading, prayer, Scripture memorization, and meditating on God's Word help by providing strength, comfort, and wisdom.  A prayer walk, an alphabetical list of blessings, and a gratitude journal are all great ways to change our focus. Ask God what He wants you to learn through your hardship. If God allows the suffering, pray that it will cause you to grow. Let the difficulties make you stronger, and if it is too much, know that He is with you and will walk with you. For me, my deteriorating health causes me to trust God more and more. While my body is decaying, my spirit is maturing.

When we seek God, He hears us and restores our strength. This is not to say that we have to pretend we are okay. I cry. It is what happens after my meltdown that matters. I have to choose not to stay in self-pity but rather pick up my cross (Matt 16:24), which is to carry my burden, and keep fighting the good fight of faith (1 Tim

6:12). Life is beyond our control. I struggle with that, but the only way to deal with our circumstances is to accept them. Sometimes we think we have achieved acceptance, but further suffering tells us differently. Faith tells us not to be disheartened because we know that God is in control, and "without faith it is impossible to please God" (Heb 11:6). We do not have to pretend that everything is fine, but we can choose to keep our suffering in perspective. God is good, and He will always take care of us.

James's words leave us to think about our reaction to suffering. Will we accept trials with joy? In each trial we undergo, perfection is being developed in us. We may not be able to see it ourselves, but it is happening. Maybe trials simply point us to the things that matter in this life, or maybe we just learn to be patient. Maybe God is calling us into deeper intimacy with Him. It could be that we have a character flaw that needs attention, or perhaps we need more humility, which suffering definitely brings. I have no doubt that faithful endurance develops Christlikeness in us.

When others watch how we handle hardships, knowing that we are Christians, it sets an example of faith. If we kick and scream and curse God, we are setting a horrible example for others and undermining the faith we claim to have. People are watching. What do we want them to think of the character of God? Don't we want them to see that He is good, even in the midst of trials? Shouldn't they know that having a relationship with Him is worthwhile?

We should be encouraged that trials work in us and grow us to completeness in Christ. He uses our circumstances to cleanse our hearts, increase our faith, develop our character, and draw us closer to Him. This is what we want to present to our sphere of influence. As I lose muscle, I try to keep moving and work out each day. The frustration is that I keep losing muscle and function despite my best efforts and commitment to exercise, and sometimes I wonder why I bother. Occasionally God sends me little reminders, like when a neighbor sees me walking with my service dog and comments that I have inspired them to exercise, or a stranger notices my struggles and admires my tenacity. These moments renew my strength. They remind me that people are watching, so my response makes a difference for me as well as influencing others. It always surprises me that if acquaintances hear about the extent of my suffering, they say that they never would have known because I seem like I'm always smiling and joyful. That comes from God. There is absolutely no other explanation.

While it is good to pray and lament to God over our situation, when we turn from Him or speak against Him, we are giving in to the temptation to sin. Our tendency is to want to give up during hardships, but if we persevere, we can watch God work in us and find joy in the testing (Matt 5:11–12; Luke 6:23). "For those who have been tried and tested, trials and afflictions are the source of the greatest joy, for that is how their faith is proved."[84] We often allow difficulties to drive a wedge between us and God through resentment and disobedience. If we wallow in our suffering, we will never grow to maturity. That is why James tells us to "let endurance have its complete effect" (1:4). This sounds like surrender to me. It may seem

---

[84] Bray and Oden, *James, 1-2 Peter, 1-3 John, Jude*, 73.

that God brings us right to the edge and we cannot handle one more little thing, but He will not push us over that edge. In actuality, when we rely on God and trust His plan, we mature and become stronger and more "complete." God is asking us to take the focus off of ourselves in favor of His plan. We are to be filled with the fruit of the Spirit—love, joy, peace, forbearance, kindness, goodness, faithfulness, gentleness and self-control (Gal 5:22–23)—which allows us to grow in the likeness of Jesus. Genesis teaches that God can bring good out of evil (Gen 50:20), and Paul teaches that God's grace is sufficient for us (2 Cor 12:9).[85] We can rely on these promises.

God did not create us to walk this life alone. He is with us in the midst of it all. Sometimes He sends people to walk alongside us that we may not have otherwise known. Perhaps we can be a light to them. We are called to share the good news of Jesus Christ. When people see my faith in spite of my worsening circumstances, they want to know how I can stay strong. I pray that my response points them to Jesus. After all, that is the Great Commission (Matt 28:18–20) of the Christian life. We do not have to be ordained ministers to share the good news of Jesus and the salvation He provides. As we serve others, it gives us a sense of joy as we become the hands and feet of Jesus. We can serve in the places that matter to our hearts. For example, I planned a gala to raise money for the Charcot-Marie-Tooth Association. It will not benefit me—I'm too far down the disease path—but it makes me happy knowing that it may help

---

[85] Blomberg and Kovalishyn, *James,* ch. 1.

someone else down the road. I also volunteered for a research project for those with eye issues due to Sjogren's Disease and autonomic dysfunction. Again, there will most likely be no benefit to me, but I hope it will help others who have these diseases to prevent progression in their eye deterioration. Serving in this way gives me a sense of joy and purpose. There are countless places where we can serve at any time, but when we are able to aid others in the midst of our own struggles, it forces our focus outward and gives us a sense of purpose.

True joy comes from knowing where we will spend eternity. "No one can take away this joy. We are tempted by adversities in order to learn the virtue of patience and faith. We are not to be discouraged by these trials. The purity of faith is made perfect by patient endurance of affliction, which casts out fear. . . . Only those who endure adversity are rewarded."[86]

We need to ask ourselves if our faith is strong enough to trust God. Does our suffering make us bitter and negative? Does it make us question God? If the answer is yes, these are the times to ask for guidance, forgiveness, wisdom, and the strength to keep going. Always remember that suffering is an opportunity to draw closer to God, and it is never too late to shift our mindset towards joy. Take heart! The suffering will end one day when Jesus returns.

---

[86] Bray and Oden, *James, 1-2 Peter, 1-3 John, Jude*, 70–71.

# The Details

## *Literary and Historical Context*

**Author:** The name James was quite common in the first century, so there has been much debate over which James is the author of the book. Possibilities include James the brother of John and the son of Zebedee; James the son of Alpheus (one of the twelve apostles); or James the half-brother of Jesus. Most conclude that it is James the half-brother of Jesus, called "James the Just" by the early church. In James 1:1 he is referred to as "James, a slave of God and the Lord Jesus Christ," suggesting a recognizable and authoritative name. This title eliminates the need for him to provide additional information, including the fact that he is the brother of Jesus, which would have also given him credibility. He is identified as the leader of the early church in Jerusalem and "viewed as the guarantor of a Jewish expression of Christianity (Acts 12:17; 21:18–25; Gal 1:19)."[87] No other James would have been as important. The writer hints at being a Palestinian Jew when he mentions the "early and late rains" (5:7), which was a weather marvel in Palestine,[88] adding evidence to his identity as Jesus's half-brother.

**Date:** If we assume that James is the half-brother of Jesus, the book would have been written sometime before his death in AD 62 or 63 and after his conversion to Christianity (1 Cor 15:7)

---

[87] Andreas J. Köstenberger, L. Scott Kellum, and Charles L. Quarles, *The Lion and the Lamb: New Testament Essentials from the Cradle, the Cross, and the Crown* (Brentwood, TN: B&H Academic, 2012), 312.

[88] Ibid., 311.

which was after AD 33. "Although James displays knowledge of the Jesus tradition, the book shows no familiarity with Matthew, Mark, Luke, or John. This is consistent with an early date. . . . The social and religious circumstances reflected in James mirror that of the Christian situation in Palestine before 70 [AD]; that is, the theology is undeveloped and the Christology understated."[89] According to Acts 12:17, the letter may have been written before the canonical Gospels before the mid-50s. That gives us a range of AD 42 to the mid-50s. It is also likely that it was written before the Jerusalem Council since it does not discuss the inclusion of Gentiles in the church (the topic of the Jerusalem Council). Therefore, it would have been before Paul's letters, which brings the date to AD 42–49.[90] Many scholars agree with this dating because they believe that James is the first book of the New Testament to be written since it shows the growing issues of the early days of the church.[91]

**Audience:** James was written to "the twelve tribes in the Dispersion" which some consider to be a symbolic reference to the Christian church, the "true Israel" who are dispersed from their real home in heaven. However, the New Testament never refers to "the twelve tribes" as the church. Some believe it addresses Christians of Jewish background, referencing the twelve sons of Jacob who became the leaders of the twelve tribes of Israel. What we know for sure is that James was writing to a

---

[89] Allison, *James*, 7.
[90] Köstenberger, Kellum, and Quarles, *The Lion and the Lamb*, 313–14.
[91] Patterson, "Letter from James," 853.

group of people who were suffering.[92] They were facing trials, suggesting that the audience was the Jews, specifically, the Jews in the Dispersion, and even more specifically, the Christian Jews who were scattered abroad. Since James identified himself as "a servant of Jesus Christ" (1:1) and referred to "believers in our glorious Lord Jesus Christ" (2:1), we can assume the audience was Christian Jews (ethnic Jews who believe in Jesus as the Messiah).[93]

**Historical Context:** Since many Jews were scattered abroad at that time, James wanted to prevent the Jewish Christians from being influenced by the habits of other nations. It can be difficult to live in a place surrounded by others who do not share your beliefs. James wanted them to stay strong, endure, and stick to their faith. After Peter left Jerusalem to start new churches, James became the leader of the church in Jerusalem. As the first Christian community, the people faced challenging times— famine, poverty, and persecution. James led the Jerusalem church with wisdom and courage until he was murdered for following Jesus around AD 62.

**Geographic Context:** Since the location of the writing is determined by which James authored the book, there are many suggestions as to where James was written. Potential locations include Rome, Egypt/Alexandria, Syria, Antioch Palestine, Jerusalem, and Galilee. If James, the half-brother of Jesus, was the author, it is believed that he never left Palestine. This would

---

[92] McCartney, Yarbrough, and Stein, *James*, 81.
[93] Patterson, "Letter from James," 852–53.

Indicate that the book was written in Jerusalem or Palestine (1:1).[94]

**Literary Context:** The topic of suffering and faith is seen throughout the Bible—both in the Old and New Testaments. James has a great deal of overlap with Job in the Old Testament in its teaching about suffering; however, their distinct perspectives on suffering show their different literary contexts. Whereas the book of Job addresses the issue of trusting God's sovereignty during suffering, James would say that God uses adversity to strengthen and purify our faith. James relies on the Old Testament Scripture in addition to Jesus's teachings to morally guide his readers.

Much can be learned about James from Paul's letters and the book of Acts (Acts 12; 15; Gal 1–2). Both men state that faith in Christ is the means for justification (Rom 3:28; Gal 2:16, 3:11), not works, according to the law. In other words, it is impossible to follow the Ten Commandments perfectly, so Jesus came to make us right with God instead. James 1:2–4 parallels 1 Peter 1:6–7 in its conversation about suffering. In ancient literature, it was common to borrow ideas from other authors and fine-tune them to suit one's own purposes. This is what James did with the Old Testament and teachings of Jesus.[95] Both Peter and James may have borrowed from common Christian teaching that circulated in the churches before the epistles were written.

---

[94] Allison, *James,* 94.

[95] Burge and Green, *The New Testament in Antiquity,* 501–2.

While Paul and Peter were troubled by the challenges of early Christian theology, James was bothered by people's deviations from true Christianity.[96] Biblical scholar Debelius' form-critical analysis considered the 'work to be a haphazard collection of disorganized, isolated, unoriginal sayings loosely connected by catchwords.'"[97] However, Fred O. Francis, who came after Debelius, recognized the literary organization in James. He considered the book to have themes of testing, wisdom, and wealth (1:2–11) with a re-presentation of those same themes (1:12–25). He considered the insertion of "eschatological instruction, thematic reprise, prayer, and health concerns in 5:12–20 to be indicative of a literary conclusion according to contemporary Hellenistic [Greek] letter-writing norms. This was a significant step beyond Debelius because it promoted the idea that James was structured as an epistle from start to finish."[98] Unlike Paul's letters that address specific issues in local churches, James shares wisdom for the entire community of Jesus's followers as general counsel without a particular situation.

**Genre and Literary Style:** The book of James is best viewed as a general letter (epistle) with pastoral advice. The first verse opens with the basics of a first-century Greco-Roman letter (sender, recipients, and greeting). From there, contrary to the earlier stated belief of Fred O. Francis, more modern thinking says it loses the traditional elements of an epistle, resembling the

---

[96] Ibid., 503.
[97] Brandell, "Discerning the Literary Structure," 230.
[98] Ibid., 230–31.

structure of wisdom literature after the initial letter opening. However, it lacks thanksgiving, a typical letter body (information and exhortation), and a closing. Instead, James starts right in on his three main themes: trials for the Christian, wisdom, and riches and poverty.[99] The book can be divided into three parts: the opening of the letter (1:1), the overview of its themes (1:2–27), and the development of those themes (2–5). The book ends without the formal closing of a typical epistle; however, each section of the book concludes its own train of thought which connects back to the introduction rather than the typical flow from one section to the next, allowing James to be considered a coherent work despite its seeming choppiness.[100] It may be its atypical structure that causes confusion about the book, rather than the themes of the book themselves.[101] While it lacks the expected occasion, mention of specific names, and traditional epistle ending,[102] the book summarizes James's wisdom for any group of Jesus's followers. James is testing the way Christians live. Some refer to the letter as "the Proverbs of the New Testament," suggesting that James is part of a genre called "wisdom *paraenesis*" since it contains many similarities to other wisdom literature[103] which typically give commands, instructions on how to live, comparisons between the wise and the foolish, and warnings. *Paraenesis* is a collection of unoriginal principles

---

[99] Blomberg and Kovalishyn, *James*, ch. 1.
[100] As quoted in Brandell, "Discerning the Literary Structure," 236.
[101] Ibid., 229.
[102] Köstenberger, Kellum, and Quarles, *The Lion and the Lamb*, 315.
[103] Brandell, "Discerning the Literary Structure," 234.

or proverbs with the purpose of giving moral instruction.[104] Much like Aesop's Fables, it tends to be more of a reminder rather than presenting new information. Usually, paraenesis restates how to live out a certain way of thinking or religion—what to do and what not to do.[105]

**Biblical Context:** Some scholars do not see much value in the book of James, yet it plays a significant role in the New Testament canon. Enhancing Paul's doctrine of justification by grace alone through faith alone, James claims that genuine faith will result in good works, otherwise it is not true faith at all. In other words, behavior follows belief. The good works will flow from our faith, a point that Jesus Himself made. (Matt 7:21).[106]

The book is absent from many canons, and Latin authorities did not acknowledge it before the last half of the fourth century because some theologians debated its emphasis on faith with accompanying action.[107] By the end of the fourth century, it reached canonical status in most Christian sectors, including in Sinaiticus and Vaticanus (two of the oldest Greek manuscripts of the Bible). The Christian theologian Augustine considered it to be authoritative scripture[108] since James was an early church leader and his message that genuine faith is proven by good works aligns with existing Christian doctrine. In 1596, one Bible was published in which James was classified among the New

---

[104] Burge and Green, *The New Testament in Antiquity*, 496.
[105] Allison, *James*, 75.
[106] Köstenberger, Kellum, and Quarles, *The Lion and the Lamb*, 310.
[107] Allison, *James*, 18.
[108] Ibid., 100.

Testament apocrypha (writings that are not accepted as part of the canon), and another was published which listed James as non-canonical. Once Catholicism and Protestantism split, James became popular among Lutherans and was commonly acknowledged as canon in the 19th century.[109] However, the book does not refer to Jesus or the Holy Spirit much, which raises questions for its placement in the traditional canon. Conversely, James shows the value in the wisdom teaching of the Old Testament since Christianity is based in Judaism.[110] Today, James is found in most versions of the Bible, making many significant contributions to the canon as an archetype of early Jewish Christianity. It shows the correlation of faith and works and the necessity of wisdom. James emphasizes Old Testament men of faith, like Job, who remained faithful during suffering (5:11), and he focuses on encouraging Christians to live humbly, controlling their tongues, and not favoring the wealthy.[111]

[109] Ibid., 103.
[110] Köstenberger, Kellum, and Quarles, *The Lion and the Lamb*, 310.
[111] Ibid., 309–10.

# Chapter 5

## WHY CAN'T IT BE MY WAY?

### Mark 14:35–36

*"Going a little farther, he fell to the ground and prayed that if possible the hour might pass from him. 'Abba, Father,' he said, 'everything is possible for you. Take this cup from me. Yet not what I will, but what you will.'"* (NIV)

Suffering has a whole separate component beyond the trials themselves. The emotional aspect can be a huge burden. My disabilities often make me feel self-conscious and inadequate. I am all for being unique, but this is not what I had in mind. Despite my best efforts, I do worry about what other people are thinking and saying about me. This causes an emotional rollercoaster every time I get ready for an event. Most people look forward to a party, choose an outfit, and enjoy socializing. For me, emotional gymnastics is involved. Will there be somewhere for me to sit so I don't fall? Will someone sit with me, or will I look like an awkward wallflower in the corner by myself? What will the weather be like? Will there be air conditioning? I have a horrible heat intolerance, so if it is too hot, I am in danger of having heat stroke. (75° F / 23.8° C is too much for

89

me.) Will I have an unexpected autonomic dysfunction episode where I get super weak, nauseous, and lightheaded with irregular heartbeats? My legs swell and then my braces dig into my calves and leave cuts. What do I wear? I am limited to outfits that accommodate my leg braces with flat shoes that are tied onto my feet so they don't fall off. I have to be careful of the way I move since my ribs can slip painfully out of place due to my Ehlers-Danlos disease. That is just mentally preparing for the party. The party itself is a whole other emotional struggle.

I have been to many parties where the ladies are all standing in a circle chit-chatting. My peripheral neuropathy (CMT) makes balance particularly challenging, so it is difficult to join in these chat circles. Talk about feeling left out! I have fallen in front of people, then laughed it off to avoid making it awkward for anyone. So embarrassing and frankly exhausting! All of this causes anxiety and depression. This is not meant to be a call for sympathy. My point is that one simple outing—a party, nonetheless!—can be emotionally taxing. How could a simple party be one of my biggest trials?

There is also the emotional suffering of the unknown. As I write this, I'm recovering from one of those autonomic dysfunction episodes. It is a sign of progression in that particular disease, so the grieving process begins again. The fear of how bad things may get creeps back in. It is the torment of knowing what is likely still to come. After my pity party, I ask God to take this suffering from me, to heal me, but I always ask for His will above mine. If it is not His will to heal me, then I need His strength to keep going. This is where my faith comes in. There is something He wants me to learn, do, or share in the suffering. Most of all, He is transforming me to be more Christlike. Nothing is too difficult for God (Gen 18:14; Jer 32:17, 27). He can heal me if that is His desire. I genuinely believe that. The greatest purpose you and I have in life is to love and serve God, so if serving Him means I suffer through all these diseases with all the accompanying emotional pain, then I will grow where He has planted me, knowing that I am doing His will. While there is nothing more I want than to escape the suffering (emotional and physical), I remind myself that God's will is being accomplished when I show up despite my limitations. It can be a difficult decision to show up to an event knowing that my health can cause me problems at any moment. One time, I attended a party that I had a feeling was going to be challenging due to the layout of the venue, but the friendship is a valuable one and I wanted to honor my friend, so I went. I came within an inch of falling backwards down a flight of stairs in view of lots of people. By the grace of God, I caught myself. As I laughed it off, I showed the other guests that my attendance was more important than my self-consciousness. My greatest purpose is most likely smack in the middle of my agony. God will be glorified, and I will grow.

I have a confession to make—I used to think, "So what?" God is glorified. Blah blah blah. How does that help me? But I have come to realize that God being glorified is the whole point. As I am filled with more of God and less of me (John 3:30), I can see more clearly. I see the point of life and the point of suffering. Once again, it is all about God, not me. Even Jesus wanted God to take away the suffering He was about to endure on the cross, but He knew the importance of following God's will. Can you imagine if God said, "Okay Jesus, never mind. Since you asked nicely, you do not need to die on the cross"? We would not have salvation. God's entire plan for humanity would have come to a screeching halt. There is a purpose for Jesus's suffering and there is for ours too. Every single trial is an opportunity to deepen our relationship with God. Suffering provides the occasion to watch God work in our lives through His comfort, mercy, strength, and wisdom. He values our loyalty to Him regardless of our circumstances. Each time I read Mark 14:35–36, I cannot begin to envision the sheer agony in Jesus's plea, which is far greater than my own experience. God did not take His suffering away, but He gave Jesus the strength to endure, and He will do the same for you and me. He has a plan, and to escape our suffering would interfere with His design.

# Setting the Scene

The entire book of Mark is about Jesus the Messiah. Can you imagine being part of the original audience? Would you have thought that Mark was crazy, delusional, making things up? Or would the Old Testament prophecies come to mind and therefore make the book seem reasonable? Jesus's own people did not recognize Him, but when Jesus died, even a Roman soldier acknowledged that "this man really was God's Son" (15:39). If you were there, would you have believed that He is the Messiah? Mark's entire Gospel was written so that everyone will know that Jesus is the Son of God, the Messiah, and the fulfillment of prophecy.

The book of Mark informs us that John the Baptist prepared the way for Jesus (1:1–13), and a voice from heaven announced Jesus to be God's "beloved Son" (1:11). Mark tells of Jesus's teachings and explains the opposition that Jesus had to suffer. He describes Jesus's endeavors (1:14–8:26) and how He proclaims God's kingdom (1:14–15). Mark details how Jesus calls His disciples, teaches people, and heals those who are suffering (1:16–45). Jesus chooses the twelve disciples (3:13–19), performs miracles (4:35–5:53), and authorizes His disciples to preach and heal as He does (6:7–8:10). Mark then recounts Jesus's journey from Caesarea Philippi to Jerusalem (8:22–10:52) as He teaches the disciples that He must suffer, die, and then rise again (8:31; 9:31; 10:33–34).

Subsequently, Mark gives us the highpoint of Jesus's mission—that Jesus, the Son of Man, came "to give his life as a ransom for many" (10:45). At the Last Supper, Jesus told the disciples that one of them would betray Him (14:12–26), and Judas did just as Jesus foretold (14:43–45). Jesus was then rejected by His own people and handed over to Pontius Pilate (the Roman ruler who presided over Jesus's trial) to be crucified (11:1–16:8). Mark 14:35–36 is part of the account in Gethsemane where Jesus goes to pray, showing His true suffering as He fights to accept God's will for Him to die on the cross. He knows He must, and He is willing to do the will of God to fulfill Scripture,[112] but it is an emotionally taxing feat.

As one of the Gospels, the book of Mark shares the Good

---

[112] John R. Donahue, and Daniel J. Harrington, Sj. *The Gospel of Mark*, Sacra Pagina, (Collegeville: Liturgical Press, 2002), 37–38.

News of Jesus Christ. It truly is good news for us because we will spend eternity in heaven, but can you relate to the emotional burden He had to bear for us? We know that Jesus was well aware of what was to come since He predicted His own death three times, but it is not just about the physical torture ahead of Him. The emotional torment and distress are so severe that His "sweat was like drops of blood falling to the ground" (Luke 22:44). As much as you and I are suffering right now, can you envision the depth of Jesus's suffering before heading for the cross?

# Overall Meaning of the Passage

The story of Jesus in the garden of Gethsemane is powerful. Jesus is exceedingly distressed and anxious knowing what He is about to endure. He is willing to lay down His life to save us, as was His Father's will, but the emotional torture of the cross is overwhelming. We cannot begin to visualize the sheer agony Jesus is facing. "Mark uses a word to suggest the greatest possible degree of horror and suffering (*ekthambeo*) in 14:33. He boldly allows us to see Jesus suffering psychological anguish before his physical suffering . . . as he faces the dreadful prospect before him. . . . He is grieved with a sorrow unto death . . . [and] it drives him to prayer."[113] Jesus clearly displays His feelings about the approaching hardship.

When He goes to Gethsemane to pray, Jesus prays that His

---

[113] David E. Garland, *Mark,* (Grand Rapids, Mich: Zondervan Academic, 1996), Mark 14:32–52.

Father might remove the cup of suffering from Him (14:35–36). Then He returns to the disciples whom He brought with Him to share in His sorrow and exclaimed, "The hour has come" (14:41). It is time for Judas's betrayal (14:41b–42). Jesus's struggle at Gethsemane plays a vital role in fulfilling God's plan of redemption. If Jesus is unsuccessful here, He cannot succeed at the cross. His willingness to obey God makes the victory at the cross possible. What a beautiful picture of love! Jesus loves His Father enough to obey Him even though the suffering would be unbearable, and He loves us enough to die for our benefit.

The only way I can even begin to relate to this is that I would literally take the heart out of my chest (suffer and die) and give it to my daughter so she could live (although there would be anesthesia and a hospital with doctors and nurses involved, so I wouldn't really suffer). I'm okay with that because I love her so much. In the same way, Jesus loves us enough to suffer and die for us, but He endures severe torture to do so (no hospital gown, no bed to lie in—just the agony of hanging from a cross). Jesus is the perfect example of love and suffering as part of God's will.

# Discussion of Individual Verses

Looking at these verses in more detail offers a better understanding of Jesus's emotional pain:

**Mark 14:35:** *"Going a little farther, he fell to the ground and prayed that if possible the hour might pass from him."*

***"He fell to the ground and prayed."*** Typically people stood to pray (Mark 11:25; Matt 6:5; Luke 18:11, 13); however, when people were in distress or suffering, they would fall facedown (Gen 17:1–3; Lev 9:24; Num 14:5; 16:4, 22, 45; 20:6; 2 Sam 12:16; Matt 17:6; Luke 5:12; 17:16; 24:5; 1 Cor 14:25), just as Jesus does here when He asks God to spare Him the suffering He is about to experience.

Jesus's prayer of lament follows the typical pattern seen in the psalms. In the Jewish lament, prayers are not "'fully controlled, or strained with politeness. In a rush of emotion, complaint, and even recrimination, the believers pour out their hearts to God.' Prayers asking God to have a change of mind are not considered insubordinate, but actually exude trust that God listens to prayer and grants requests that can be reconciled 'with overall Providence.'"[114]

***"If possible."*** This comment doesn't even make sense in our mortal definition of the phrase. Is there anything God cannot do? Of course not. Nothing lies outside the scope of His power, and Jesus knows this. "If possible" must be interpreted through the lens of God's omnipotence (9:23; 10:27; 14:36) since God is not bound by the laws

---

[114] Ibid.

of nature. Absolutely nothing can limit Him. The question is not one of God's ability; rather, it is an appeal. Jesus knows that God *can* remove the "hour" and the "cup," so He is hoping that God will change His sovereign plan. This is not an uncommon theme in biblical prayer.[115] Jesus doesn't want to let humanity suffer, but He is hoping there might be another way to provide salvation. "He is showing the weakness that belongs to human nature. Human nature would prefer not to be torn from the present life. It would draw back and shrink from death . . . because God has implanted in human nature love for the life of this world."[116]

***"The hour."*** The "hour" refers to that moment of Jesus's death, but it also seems to refer to the end of times (13:32). "Early Christians like Mark regarded Jesus's death and resurrection as the decisive moment toward the full coming of God's kingdom. . . . The suffering and crucifixion of Jesus are a physical trial for him, but also part of a cosmic struggle."[117] This struggle is what this passage is all about—the emotional agony that accompanies the physical torture in front of Jesus.

***"Might pass from him."*** This painful fate is one He wants to avoid, so He is praying for an alternative plan.

**Mark 14:36:** *"'Abba, Father'" he said, 'everything is possible for you. Take this cup from me. Yet not what I will, but what you will.'"*

***"Abba, Father."*** This is how Jesus addresses God. It is a term that

---

[115] Donahue and Harrington, *Mark*, 477.

[116] Thomas C. Oden, and Christopher A. Hall, eds., *Mark: Volume 2* (Westmont: InterVarsity Press, 2005), 374.

[117] Donahue and Harrington, *Mark*, 477.

displays His intimate relationship with His Father. "Father" here denotes God's protection, wisdom, guidance, and authority. The Lord's Prayer is addressed this way as well (Luke 11). This name includes the actual Aramaic term Jesus used for God (*'abbā'*) and its Greek translation. This is not the way to address an impersonal or uninvolved individual. Actually, it is because of their close personal relationship as Father and Son that Jesus knows He can pray to God this way.[118] In the same way, believers know they can cry out to God because they are adopted into His family (Ps 89:27; Rom 8:15; 9:4).[119]

***"Everything is possible for you."*** Jesus restates His comment "if possible" (14:35) to provide reassurance about His faith that God can do anything. He also reiterates His statement that "all things are possible with God" (10:27 NIV). Jesus knows that if there is any other way, God will change the plan, but this is the only way. There is no choice but for Jesus to drink the cup of suffering. If He had not, we would not have eternal life. That would have ruined the weaving of the tapestry for sure.

***"Take this cup from me."*** The "cup" refers to Jesus's suffering.[120] Jesus shows His human weakness through His intense distress and suffering when He asks for the "cup" to be taken away. He teaches patience in suffering by becoming patient in suffering Himself.[121] Rather than taking the "cup" of suffering from Him, God gives Him

---

[118] Robert H. Stein, *Mark (Baker Exegetical Commentary on the New Testament)*, (Grand Rapids: Baker Academic, 2008), 662.

[119] Thomas Scott Caulley, "The Place of Abba in Mark's Christology," *Bulletin for Biblical Research* 32, no. 4 (2022): 396.

[120] Donahue and Harrington, *Mark*, 478.

[121] Oden and Hall, *Mark*, 372.

the strength to drink the cup. What exactly is in this "cup"?

> [It] involves giving his life as a ransom for many (10:45) and his sacrificially pouring out his blood to seal the new covenant (14:24). It is not the physical suffering he will have to endure that troubles Jesus. Rather, it is that he would become sin for us even though he knew no sin (2 Cor 5:21) and a curse for us all (Gal 3:13) that we might escape the wrath of God. He feared the death that no one else would ever need to or be able to experience. He would experience God's wrath in order that those who believe in Him would not have to face it.[122]

This cup is full of sin—all the sin ever committed by humankind, starting with Adam and Eve and continuing until Jesus returns. That thing you did yesterday. . . . it's in there too. None of the sin in that cup was committed by Jesus. He is perfect (1 Pet 1:18–19; 2:22; Heb 4:15; 1 John 3:5), yet He had to drink the cup and become the sin that was in that cup (2 Cor 5:21)—and the suffering from drinking that cup is unimaginable.

The cup is also full of God's wrath and judgment against sin —our sin. Holy and just, God does not tolerate sin.[123] Someone must pay the consequences for sinful humanity, so Jesus becomes the One who drinks the cup of the Father's anger so that you and I do not have to drink from that cup. Is this the only way? Yes. Otherwise, God would have a different plan. But He does not need a backup plan. God's plans are perfect. Jesus "does not pray that the cup may pass around Him. He prays that the cup may pass away from Him,

---

[122] Stein, *Mark*, 661–63.
[123] Garland, *Mark*, Mark 14:32–52.

but it cannot pass away unless He drinks it. To pass away, does not mean to depart from its place, but not to exist at all."[124] Jesus prays to be rescued from death; but "instead he will be delivered through death and glorified by the resurrection."[125]

***"Yet not what I will, but what you will."*** Although Jesus desperately wants to avoid the suffering He is about to undergo, He still submits to the will of God. Notice how Jesus says, "yet" not my will and "but" your will. This doubling up "adds to the power of Jesus' statement. It also serves as the basis for the doctrine that Jesus had both a human and a divine will. . . . The final words of Jesus' prayer echo petition in Matthew's version of the Lord's prayer (Matt 6:10: 'Thy will be done') and here expresses his perfect acceptance of the cross as God's will."[126] After praying to God and presenting His own will, Jesus accepts God's will and faces the "hour" and the "cup." This type of prayer displays great faith and trust in God and His sovereignty. To say "but what you will" means to surrender your own personal agenda. Jesus recognizes that this is the only way to accomplish God's plan for salvation, otherwise His sacrificial death would not have been necessary.

---

[124] Oden and Hall, *Mark*, 376.
[125] Garland, *Mark*, Mark 14:32–52.
[126] Donahue and Harrington, *Mark*, 477–78.

# Theological Reflections

Mark's theology is the good news of God (1:14), and Jesus is the Son of God (1:1). A major theme in the book of Mark is the messianic secret: Jesus knows He is the Messiah, but He tries to keep it a secret in the first half of the book. Later, He reveals His identity to His disciples but insists they not tell anyone (8:27–30). His messiahship could only be revealed after His death and resurrection (9:9).[127] Even the demons know who Jesus is but are commanded not to tell (1:34; 3:12). It is the same with those He heals (1:43–45). The secret reaches its peak when the Roman centurion declares at Jesus's death, "Surely this man was the Son of God!" (15:39).

The main part of Mark's theology is the kingdom of God (4:1–34), "that moment when all creation will acknowledge the sovereignty of God and proceed according to God's original plan"[128] (Gen 1:26–28). He addresses discipleship and the cost to follow Jesus (8:34–9:1; 9:33–10:31).[129] He includes the disciples' failures as well: Peter denied Jesus; Judas betrayed Him; and the rest of the disciples abandoned Him (chs. 14–15). If the disciples could not understand Jesus as Messiah, His mission on earth, and the significance of the cross, they would not comprehend their own charge to deny their personal desires and commit to following Jesus's teaching. They had to be willing to suffer for His sake (8:34). Mark's theology also incorporates the coming of the Son of Man

---

[127] W. R. Telford, *The Theology of the Gospel of Mark* (Cambridge: Cambridge University Press, 1999), 47.

[128] Donahue and Harrington, *Mark*, 53.

[129] Ibid., 34.

(13), emphasizing that disciples are to follow Jesus and mimic Him, which includes service, surrender, sacrifice, and suffering.

## Pointing to Jesus

The entire book of Mark is about Jesus. "It is not just a collection of stories about Jesus; his book tells the story of Jesus as a whole."[130] Mark describes Jesus in many ways:

> He appears as an authoritative teacher (1:21–22), a charismatic prophet (8:27–28) and a popular healer and exorcist (1:32–34). He is described as the "Nazarene" [from Nazareth] (10:47) and addressed as "Teacher" (4:34), "Rabbi" (9:5), or "Lord" (7:28). He is acclaimed as the "Holy One of God" (1:24), greeted as the "Son of David" (10:47) and confessed as "Christ" (8:29) or "Son of God" (15:39). He speaks of himself, however, as the "Son of Man" and defines his role as that of a servant (10:45).[131]

Mark wants his readers to understand who Jesus is, so he discusses the miracles of Jesus: healing (1:29–31, 40–45; 2:1–12; 3:1–6; 5:25–34; 7:31–37; 8:22–26; 10:46–52), resurrection from the dead (5:21–24, 35–40, 43), and exorcism (1:21–28; 5:1–13; 7:24–30; 9:14–29). In addition, he names natural miracles: calming of a storm (4:35–41), feeding five thousand people with five loaves of bread and two fish (6:35–44), walking on the sea (6:45–54), feeding four thousand people with very little (8:1–9), and cursing a fig tree that later withered (11:12–14, 20–25).[132] "His miracles are more than

---

130 Rodney Reeves, "Gospel of Mark," in Brand, *Holman Illustrated Bible Dictionary,* 1056.

131 Telford, *The Theology of the Gospel of Mark,* 30.

132 Stein, *Mark,* 21–22.

indications of his power; they are incidents in his ministry which reflect and clarify the nature of his person."[133]

Mark also gives examples of Jesus's teachings:

> He claims the divine prerogative of forgiving sins (2:5–12; cf. Luke 7:36–50), that one's eternal destiny depends on following Him (Mark 8:34–38; 9:37–42; 10:28–31; 12:6–12; 13:9–13), that he has authority over the Sabbath (2:23–28; 3:1–6). . . . He claims that with His coming, the kingdom of God has arrived (Mark 1:14–15; 2:18–20, 21–22; 14:22–24; cf. 3:23–27) and provides a symbolic act illustrating this by appointing twelve disciples (3:13–19) to indicate that in his ministry, God is bringing about the restoration of the twelve tribes of Israel.[134]

Jewish theology in the Old Testament days expected resurrection to be an end-times occurrence (Dan 12:1–3), but some scholars question whether Mark has his own Christology (the part of theology that concerns Jesus) or if he merely combines the viewpoints of others.[135] Scholars believe that Mark's story is the first to discuss the resurrection of Jesus.[136] Mark's message is summarized in Mark 1:15 when Jesus announces, "The time has come. . . . The kingdom of God has come near. Repent and believe the good news!" (NIV). This puts the story into an end-times context, including the themes of demonic conflict and humanity's rejection of Jesus; however,[137] the ultimate victory belongs to Jesus

---

[133] Heber F. Peacock, "Theology of the Gospel of Mark," *Review & Expositor* 55, no. 4 (1958): 395.

[134] Stein, *Mark*, 22.

[135] Telford, *The Theology of the Gospel of Mark*, 32.

[136] Donahue and Harrington, *Mark*, 53.

[137] Peacock, "Theology of the Gospel of Mark," 397.

through the cross. It is through faith in Him that you and I can claim that victory. Why? Because He suffered by drinking from the "cup" that saved us, just as God had planned.

# Application

We must believe that Jesus is the Son of God (1:1), and when we identify with Him, we need to be ready to carry our cross and suffer too (8:34–38). Carrying our cross means persevering in our trials and burdens. It is a denial of our own will in exchange for God's will. Jesus died as a ransom for our sins (10:45), something we could not do on our own. He paid a great price for us. Jesus suffered immense physical and emotional torture on earth and look at Him now! He is sitting at the right hand of the Father (Heb 1:3; 8:1; 12:2; Mark 14:62; 16:19; Eph 1:20–21; Rom 8:34; Col 3:1; 1 Pet 3:22; Acts 7:55–56). How did He get there? He surrendered His will to God's will and acknowledged the authority of His Father. By submitting to God's authority, we are acknowledging that we are not the authority. If God could achieve His purposes differently, then He would take our hardships away. Your specific hardship is part of God's plan. In His divine wisdom, God made each of us unique, so there are certain contributions you can make to the world that I cannot and vise-versa.

If God calls us to endure agony, we have the opportunity to prove our love and gratitude for Him. There is no better place to be than smack in the middle of God's will. This is where we can glorify God and be a blessing to others. That is why we were created—to glorify God. What does it mean to glorify God? We worship Him for who He is, honoring His nature and characteristics rather than focusing on what He can do for us. True fulfillment comes from loving, serving, and obeying Him. It is a simple (but, again, not easy) tweak in our perspective. If we are here to serve ourselves, we will never have peace. When we live to glorify God, our suffering makes more sense. The suffering does not go away, but we can find joy in it knowing that we can glorify God through our trials. As we do, others will see the hope we have and glorify God too. Our suffering is a major part of our impact and purpose, but we can only have peace and be joyful in the midst of our suffering if we submit to God's authority, surrender our will, obey God, and carry our own cross. Trust that the tapestry He is weaving will be beautiful.

Jesus's prayer shows us how we can articulate our anxiety while surrendering to God's will in the end. The best thing we can do is pray for God's will and the strength to endure our suffering on earth. Can you pray like this? Let's try:

Dear Lord, you know that I am suffering with ___________ (fill in your hardship). I ask that you would take ___________ away, but only if it is your will. If not, I ask that you walk with me and give me the strength to endure. Amen.

The overall concept of this passage is that we are to submit to God's authority. It is a voluntary and willing obedience to God—not a sad or angry surrender. Releasing our will to God is an active compliance, not a passive or apathetic inaction. It is not simply giving up. If our will is different than God's will, we are to choose His over our own. If we are ever unclear, we need to search His Word. To achieve God's will, we must be willing to suffer. Why should we submit to His will? Because we love God. We love God because He first loved us (1 John 4:19). Jesus says that we show our love when we obey His commandments (John 14:15). Christ surrendered His will for us to spend eternity with God. This is something we could never accomplish on our own. The only way for us to be forgiven is through Jesus's horrible death on the cross. If there was any other way, then God would have taken the cup of suffering away from Jesus. As such, Jesus is the only way for us to get to heaven.

It has taken me a while to understand that this is how life works as a child of God. I admit that I fall short sometimes, but my heart is turned toward God and His will. My diseases started over forty years ago, and it has taken me that long to see the unique purpose of my pain, but I now believe it is to author this book to share with you. If I can help you to see that surrendering your will in exchange for God's superior will and purpose is the way to manage hardships, then I believe I will have served the purpose of my suffering. What a great purpose! So say it with me: "His will be done."

# The Details

## Literary and Historical Context

The Gospel of Mark has the shortest narrative of Jesus's ministry. Mark's goal was to take the oral tradition and put it in writing. Mark's Gospel is not unique like the other gospels: It matches about 90 percent of Matthew, about 48 percent of Luke, and about 95 percent of Matthew and Luke combined, but it is thought that Matthew and Luke used Mark as the main source for their gospels. Similar to the pattern of Peter's preaching, Mark's Gospel is a quick portrayal of the life of Jesus highlighting Jesus as the Son of God. Rather than concentrating on the parables of Jesus, Mark emphasizes Jesus's miracles.[138]

**Author:** Despite its title, Mark is an anonymous work. Scholars agree that it was written by a Greek-speaking Gentile living outside Palestine, possibly in Rome. The author does not name himself or declare himself to be a firsthand eyewitness to the events described. This way the focus is on Jesus, not the author. The heading "according to Mark" is not part of the original work but was added later in keeping with the early church's custom.[139] Mark is the narrator and implied author (where the author is understood from reading the narrative). "The concept of the implied author focuses on the 'intention' of the text rather than on the . . . . actual person who wrote the book."[140]

---

[138] Köstenberger, Kellum, Quarles, *The Lion and the Lamb*, 77.
[139] Donahue and Harrington, *Mark*, 54.
[140] Ibid., 34–35.

Most believe the author is John Mark, who was usually called by his Greek name, Mark. He is the cousin of the early Christian leader Barnabas (Col 4:10), and he is a companion of Barnabas and Paul on their first missionary journey. On the second missionary journey, Barnabas wants Mark to come along, but Paul does not because Mark had left them on the first journey, causing a rift between Paul and Barnabas (Acts 15:39). Later, however, Paul leaves the impression that Mark is with him (Col 4:10; Phil 24; 2 Tim 4:11), indicating that they had reconciled. Mark is known as Peter's interpreter, and Peter calls Mark his "son" (indicating a spiritual relationship) who was with him in Rome (1 Pet 5:13). Early church figures acknowledge that Mark's work is based on Peter's preaching.[141] Since Peter was an apostle, Mark would have had firsthand knowledge of Jesus. Early tradition supports Markan authorship which would indicate that Mark interpreted Peter's memories of Jesus with great accuracy.[142]

**Date:** The Gospel of Mark is the oldest gospel, with most agreeing that it was written during the decade AD 60s.[143] However, three main possibilities exist for when Mark was written: (1) mid-50s to early 60s AD based on Peter's presence in Rome in the 50s[144] which also supports Markan priority; (2) mid-60s shortly before or shortly after Peter's murder during the

---

[141] Bill Warren, "John Mark," in Brand, *Holman Illustrated Bible Dictionary*, 1057.

[142] Oden and Hall, *Mark*, 44–45.

[143] Donahue and Harrington, *Mark*, 57.

[144] Köstenberger, Kellum, and Quarles, *The Lion and the Lamb*, 78.

Neronian persecution in AD 64–68;[145] or (3) late 60s to early 70s closer to the destruction of the Jerusalem Temple in AD 70. This would suggest that Mark knew about the destruction after it occurred rather than from Jesus's prophecy, which would mean that Mark was written between AD 65 and 75.[146]

**Audience:** The majority of Mark's readers would have spoken Greek but not Hebrew or Aramaic. Mark explains Jewish customs and translates words to help his readers understand (3:17; 5:41; 7:1–4, 11, 34; 15:22, 34) even though they are already familiar with the Old Testament and Christian traditions about Jesus. Since Mark's original audience was Gentiles who already knew about Jesus, he did not need to include Jesus's genealogy in his writing. The audience may have been Roman Christians,[147] which is also supported by Mark's use of Latin. This indicates a Roman origin or at least a place centered on Roman culture,[148] but Mark's overall audience is all Christians.

**Historical Context:** Rome was in a state of civil unrest at a time when additional civil and international wars were occurring. After being mostly ignored until AD 64, the church was in crisis during the reign of Nero, the Roman emperor who became infamous for persecuting Christians. The Jewish rebellion against Rome in AD 66 was initially successful, but then "the formidable Roman army made its way through Galilee with its scorched earth policy and

---

[145] Reeves, "Gospel of Mark," 1055.

[146] James A. Brooks, *Mark: An Exegetical and Theological Exposition of Holy Scripture* (Nashville: B&H, 1991), 26–27.

[147] Reeves, "Gospel of Mark," 1055.

[148] Burge and Green, *The New Testament in Antiquity*, 231–32.

by the time Mark wrote had either besieged Jerusalem (AD 69) or recently sacked the city and burned the temple to the ground (AD 70)."[149] It was rumored that the fire had been part of Nero's unpopular urban renewal plan, but to deflect attention away from himself, Nero blamed Christians for starting the fire since most Romans were already suspicious of them. This way, he was able to use the Christians as his scapegoat.[150] This is the same concept of false witness as when the Jewish leaders looked for evidence to have Jesus killed. They couldn't find any real proof, so they turned to false witnesses who lied about Jesus's statement that He would destroy and build another temple in three days (14:55–59). Jesus had already predicted the destruction of the temple but asserted that the end is still to come (13:7, 20, 27).

**Geographic Context:** Jesus's ministry covered Galilee to Judea. He was in Caesarea Philippi (8:27), Bethany (14:3), Jerusalem (14:13), the Mount of Olives (14:26), Galilee (14:28), and Gethsemane (14:32). In Aramaic, Gethsemane means "oil press," which refers to a particular place on the Mount of Olives with olive trees where the neighborhood olives were crushed for oil. John describes it as a "garden" (John 18:1) that Jesus frequently visited (John 18:2; Luke 22:39).[151] This is where Jesus went to pray for the removal of the "cup."

---

[149] Garland, *Mark*, Introduction.
[150] Ibid.
[151] Stein, *Mark*, 659–60.

**Literary Background:** The fast-paced, dramatic story of Mark is reminiscent of the dramatic features of Hellenistic (Greek) theater.[152] "Mark shares many characteristics with the oral literature of antiquity. In this sense, Mark is similar to a symphony, which is 'composed' and often draws on motives from earlier traditions and integrates different themes."[153] With mostly simple sentences, Mark uses quotations and impressions from the Old Testament to show that the coming of Jesus fulfills Old Testament prophecy that God would send His Son.[154] Mark's narratives possess a quality that makes readers feel as if they are present in the story. Additionally, Mark portrays Jesus with great authenticity[155] and reports the historical events with accuracy. Mark's typical style reflects storytelling as he joins one sentence to another using the word "and," creating quick scene changes. This style gives the book a sense of urgency.[156] Mark also uses the literary feature of repetition to highlight important elements.[157] The storyline is often disrupted by an alternate but similar narrative before it continues, known as framing or bracketing (14:11–15:39).[158] Framing is used to influence the reader's understanding of the story while bracketing is used for clarification or editorial commentary.

---

152 Burge and Green, *The New Testament in Antiquity*, 230.
153 Donahue and Harrington, *Mark*, 30.
154 Köstenberger, Kellum, and Quarles, *The Lion and the Lamb*, 80–81.
155 Donahue and Harrington, *Mark*, 30–31.
156 Ibid., 31.
157 Ibid., 32.
158 Ibid., 31–32.

**Structure and Organization:** Mark's Gospel is written as a story in chiasms in the ABB'A' pattern in which concepts are repeated in reverse order. By putting words or ideas in the opposite order in the second half of a passage, the main ideas are emphasized. Mark uses a model that repeats three times and gets more intense with each use to drive his point home. For example, Jesus calls or commissions the disciples three times (1:16–20; 3:13–19; 6:7–13); Jesus predicts His death three times (8:31; 9:31; 10:33–34); Jesus tells His disciples to keep watch three times (14:32–42); and Peter denied Jesus three times (14:66–72).

Mark's objective is to show Jesus as the Messiah as he narrates the events leading to His resurrection.[159] To that end, he writes Jesus's story in two main sections. First Jesus is shown as the powerful Messiah (1:1–8:26). The book opens with the beginnings of Jesus's ministry, then follows Him to Galilee, Caesarea Philippi, and Jerusalem. In the second part, Jesus is seen as the suffering servant (8:27–16:8). Within three chapters, Jesus teaches the apostles how He must die, the authorities plot His execution, and He dies. Women come to the tomb with burial spices to anoint Jesus's body, but Jesus is not there. The angels proclaim that He has risen showing His ultimate victory over death. After rejection, suffering, and death, the narrative ends with Christ's resurrection.

Mark is structured around three motifs: Jesus as prophet, Jesus as the recipient and mediator of God's presence, and Jesus

---

[159] Ibid., 28.

as Son of God. First, let's look at Jesus as prophet. When Jesus asks Peter, "Who do people say that I am?" (8:27), Peter responds (8:28) that people say He is a prophet (claiming that Jesus is John the Baptist, Elijah, or another of the prophets). When Jesus asks Peter, "But who do you say that I am?" Peter replies, "You are the Messiah" (8:29 NIV).[160] This changes the disciples' understanding, so they realize that calling Him a prophet is insufficient, but the crowds still do not understand and so persecute Him.

The second main motif refers to the heavens being torn open (1:10; "opened" in Matt 3:16; Luke 3:21. See Isa 64:1), thus allowing Jesus to be the recipient and mediator of God's presence. This "tearing open" of the heavens is echoed in Mark 15:38, where the veil of the temple was torn in two upon Jesus's death. "This tearing of the curtain symbolizes the new eschatological opening of believers' access to heaven/God through Jesus's ministry, made possible by his death. Jesus is thus recognized as both the recipient of God's end-time immanence and the facilitator of that closeness for his followers."[161] We see this in Jesus's teaching about His own death and the new covenant, healing of the relationship between God and humanity, and miracles showing God's power at work. It also points to the resurrection and Jesus's ultimate victory over death.

---

[160] Caulley, "The Place of Abba," 401.
[161] Ibid., 403.

The third motif is seen at the transfiguration where Jesus's appearance becomes radiant and God declares Him to be the "Son of God" and therefore superior to both Moses and Elijah (9:2–8).[162] This reveals Jesus's divine nature and anticipates His resurrection and future glory. The book has four interrelated purposes, focusing on Jesus's identity as "Son of God:"

1. A pastoral purpose: to teach Christians about the nature of discipleship
2. A missionary-training purpose: to explain how Jesus prepared his followers to take on His mission and to show others how to do so as well
3. An apologetic [defense of the faith] purpose: to demonstrate to non-Christians that Jesus is the Son of God because of His great power despite his crucifixion
4. An anti-imperial purpose: to show that Jesus, not Caesar [Roman emperor], is the true Son of God, Savior, and Lord.[163]

**Genre and Literary Style:** The book of Mark is read as a "pastoral response to stressful times."[164] As the first gospel to be written, called Markan priority, Mark created its own genre. Mark describes the genre in the first verse as "The beginning of the good news about Jesus the Messiah" (1:1 NIV). Mark thus created the "gospel" genre, which was then copied by Matthew, Luke, and authors of apocryphal gospels.[165] This "gospel" genre has some qualities of a biography, narrating the life of Jesus with the purpose of influencing the reader's behavior. Alternatively,

---

[162] Ibid., 402.
[163] Köstenberger, Kellum, and Quarles, *The Lion and the Lamb*, 80.
[164] Garland, *Mark*, Introduction.
[165] Donahue and Harrington, *Mark*, 27.

other scholars suggest that Mark copies popular Greek novels and romances, Greek tragedy, or Greco-Roman rhetorical forms.[166] Biblical narrative, the intentional telling of real events in the Bible to tell a bigger story of God's plan to save humanity, has also been suggested as a genre.[167]

Stylistically, Mark has been called the "Gospel of action" since it is so fast-paced. Mark frequently uses the word "immediately" to show that Jesus is always moving around. Mark seems more interested in Jesus's work than in His words. He leaves out things like Jesus's teaching at the Sermon on the Mount, and Mark's geographical references are only mentioned to show the widespread area of Jesus's ministry.[168] Mark uses everyday conversational Greek in sharing his message.[169] He is very detailed in transmitting the words of Jesus, along with "the reaction of the crowds, facial expressions of conversationalists, conclusions drawn by the disciples, and private remarks made by opponents (5:40; 10:22, 32, 41; 11:31: 14:40)"[170] as only an insider could do.

**Biblical Context:** Mark considered the Jewish Scriptures to be authoritative (1:2–3), so he writes the story of Jesus to present Him as the fulfillment of God's plan. He shows Jesus as the realization of Old Testament prophecy as he recounts Malachi 3:1 and Isaiah 40:3 about the coming of John the Baptist (1:2–3); he

---

[166] Ibid., 28.
[167] Ibid., 29.
[168] Reeves, "Gospel of Mark," 1055.
[169] Ibid., 1055.
[170] Ibid., 1056.

refutes the Jewish assertions that Jesus could not be the Messiah; and he shows Jesus quoting Psalm 22 on the cross (15:34), displaying God's cohesive plan as seen throughout the canon.

The book meets the requirements for canonicity: apostolicity, orthodoxy, and catholicity. It clearly shows apostolicity (written by an apostle or someone close to an apostle) since Mark was Peter's interpreter and would have heard about Jesus directly from the apostle Peter. The book meets the requirement of orthodoxy (agreeing with other books that have been accepted as authoritative); and it confirms its catholicity (being accepted by the universal church).

Mark also contributes to the canon in the following ways:

1. [He presents] a gospel of Jesus, narrating his ministry from Galilee to Jerusalem.
2. [He shows that] Jesus is the miracle-working Son of God (1:1,11; 5:7; 9:7; 15:39).
3. [He details that] Jesus is displaying his power over nature, demons, sickness, and death (4:35–5:43).
4. [He shows] discipleship failure [inability to see, hear and understand who Jesus is (Isa 6:10; Mark 4:12; 6:52; 7:14; 8:17–8) and how they deserted Jesus in his hour of need (14:50)].
5. [He presents] Jesus' sacrificial vicarious death [as] a ransom for many (10:45).[171]
6. He presents the greatest story of passion (Jesus's suffering, betrayal, trial, and crucifixion).

Mark's passion story defends the crucified Messiah, and it serves to encourage and provide hope to those suffering with their own trials.

---

[171] Köstenberger, Kellum, and Quarles, *The Lion and the Lamb*, 76.

Chapter 6

# WHY DO WE NEED GOD'S GRACE?

## 2 Corinthians 12:7–10

*"Or because of these surpassingly great revelations. Therefore, in order to keep me from becoming conceited, I was given a thorn in my flesh, a messenger of Satan, to torment me. Three times I pleaded with the Lord to take it away from me. But he said to me, "My grace is sufficient for you, for my power is made perfect in weakness." Therefore I will boast all the more gladly about my weaknesses, so that Christ's power may rest on me. That is why, for Christ's sake, I delight in weaknesses, in insults, in hardships, in persecutions, in difficulties. For when I am weak, then I am strong."* (NIV)

Have you ever looked in the mirror and thought, "Wow, I look good today"? That is not a common occurrence for me nowadays. I mean, my rosacea makes my skin look like that of a broken-out teenager combined with the wrinkles of my actual age. Shouldn't that be illegal? After growing up as a chubby kid and finally losing some weight (a battle I still struggle with), at twenty years old (and pre-diseases), I thought I looked pretty good. I was popular, and it went to my head. I was arrogant and put my confidence in my own appearance. God is not a fan of our self-importance. He wants us to be humble and remember that all good things come from Him (Jas 1:17). Our arrogance does not serve God. He cannot work through a heart that is self-serving rather than one that is turned toward Him.

How does He get us to turn our stubborn hearts? One way is by allowing us to have a "thorn in the flesh." Have you ever had a splinter in your finger? No matter how small, it hurts! We want to get rid of it. We all have "thorns"—something that bothers us, some imperfection, pain, or limitation. What if you ask God to take your thorn away and He says no? Does it make you question God's goodness? Do you wonder why a good God would allow you to suffer?

With my unfortunate concoction of diseases, you cannot look at me and think I am "normal." My imperfections are there for everyone to see. They scream, "Hey! Look at me! I am different!" Enter self-consciousness again. While my diseases are not generally life threatening (except maybe my aortic aneurism), they cause so much hardship. With each one being a separate progressive disease, it is as if my "thorn" keeps digging deeper and deeper into my flesh. Just to give you a small idea, this is my daily routine:

- First, my mornings start with all sorts of eye issues the minute I wake up, including hemorrhaging of my eyeball.
- Next, I take lots of medications and eye drops to get rolling. And this is before I am even out of bed!
- Once I am up, I put on my compression stockings since my lower legs don't pump the blood back up to my heart very well. Then I put on my leg braces and begin my daily physical therapy routine to try to hold onto my ever-decreasing strength. I go for walks with my service dog who

helps me balance, but if it is over 75°F, I start to overheat since my body can't regulate temperature, and sometimes I have episodes of weakness, nausea, lightheadedness, and racing heartbeat.

- Next, I swim, ride a stationary bike, and do Pilates or weights. By the end of all this, I'm exhausted.
- After some rest, it's time for more medications.
- The day ends with even more medications and a battle with itching-induced insomnia, just to wake up and start the process over.

It goes on and on, consuming my life. I have no energy left for anything else. While I know there are people who have it much worse than I do, my point is that I understand "thorns" and "torment." Through my thorns I have learned a great deal about myself and God. It is this weakness that keeps me humble and reliant on Him. He has rid me of my arrogance; however, he will not remove the things that keep me submissive until Jesus returns and makes all things new (2 Cor 5:17; Rev 21:5), including our bodies. New body? Yes, please! I cannot even begin to imagine eternity without leg braces. I will be the one up there dancing in heels! In the meantime, I limp around in leg braces that literally dig into my skin with the constant reminder of the "thorn in my flesh" and the humility that comes with it. It brings me to my knees (literally when I fall and figuratively).

Boasting in our weakness can feel unnatural. I do not usually run around saying, "I limp. I am weak. But glory be to God." However, this is what Paul does. Maybe we should try that too. I do, however, try to say that we all have something to deal with, and we all have blessings too. For me, my health is weak, but my marriage is strong. Someone else may have a weak marriage and strong finances. Others may have solid finances but horrible addictions. You get the idea. The point is that when we can accept our weaknesses and focus on our blessings, we will have more peace and joy and be better able to serve God.

God can do His work through me when I am meek, but I am useless to Him in my arrogance. He does not want us to rely on ourselves, our talents, our appearance, or our anything else. That is meaningless to Him. The Bible tells us that "The LORD does not look at the things people look at. People look at the outward appearance, but the LORD looks at the heart" (1 Sam 16:7 NIV). My attitude has changed from "God, I do not want to do this anymore" to "Oh, I see that you have a plan here." I have had to let go of what I thought my life would look like. The journey has not been easy, but it is worthwhile. I still grieve and struggle, but slowly God has been answering the question of "Why me?" and it makes sense when I take the bird's-eye view instead of focusing on myself. Remember, it's not about you and me; it's about God.

My friend gave me another way of looking at life on earth. She said that God has created us as spiritual beings who are on a human journey. We are not human beings on a spiritual journey. When I look at it this way, I realize that my body is just the housing for my spirit. If I went to the body store and picked one out, is this the one I would have chosen? No! But this is the one God chose for me, weaknesses and all. He knows which flaws He can best use for my good and His glory. I promise you that there is not a single perfect body in the body store! If I had yours or you had mine, could we be as useful for God? I'm guessing that the answer is no. So rather than complaining in our suffering, we can ask God what purpose He has for us in these specific bodies. Paul was given a "thorn," but after asking God for healing to no avail, he realized that his weaknesses allowed him to rely on God. Maybe our specific brand of suffering is exactly what will best serve someone else for the kingdom of God. We need an attitude adjustment to see from God's perspective.

We may view "normal" and "perfect" as the means for joy. "If I could just get rid of this suffering, I would be happy." Do you really believe that, deep down? My initial reaction is yes, but experience tells me differently. Is that where true and lasting joy comes from? Can we not rejoice while suffering? When we learn joy in the midst of suffering and when we understand our value in Christ, the struggle to be "normal" ceases. That is when we can be truly content. We have to have faith in God, not in ourselves. Self-sufficiency is a sin, whereas God-sufficiency is at the core of Christianity. Sometimes God allows suffering specifically to keep us reliant upon Him. We may think we are more valuable to God without our "thorns," but maybe those thorns are instead our superpower with which we honor Him.

As 2 Corinthians opens, the Corinthian church is divided and fighting. The book talks about Paul's relationship with the Corinthian church, his apostolic ministry, his suffering, and his anxiety about the well-being of the church in Jerusalem. Since this church is important to Paul (1 Cor 4:14–15; 2 Cor 12:15), he is adamant about restoring his relationship with them through letters and visits. "The letter overflows with tears, joy, tales of arduous journeys, suffering, stern words about boasting, and other pointed warnings—all for the sake of the gospel. . . . Paul's goal is full reconciliation for the church—first with God and also with himself (2 Cor 5:11–6:13)."[172] Paul seeks to inspire the Corinthians and confirm that they will be sending their offering to help the church in Jerusalem. He also has to deal with the "super-apostles" who have infiltrated the church and disputed Paul's apostolic authority.

Paul wants the Corinthians to know that he forgives them after a "painful visit" the last time he was there. The pain comes as the result of the Corinthians' rejection of Paul as a trustworthy leader (2 Cor 10–11) compared to the standards of the wealthier and more dramatic leaders ("super-apostles") of the time who saw this as a weakness that betrayed Paul's claim to be an apostle. Apostles were judged by their appearance rather than by recognizing the authority given by God (2 Cor 10:7–11).[173] This had a negative impact on the way the Corinthians viewed Paul. He shows them that this is not a

---

[172] Burge and Green, *The New Testament in Antiquity*, 388.
[173] Ibid.

valid value system and is an affront to Jesus. Rather than appearing arrogant, Paul is humble, placing the focus on Jesus. He wants them to understand the glory of the New Covenant in Jesus in comparison to the old covenant made through Moses (the Ten Commandments). The old covenant was written on stone tablets with a temporary nature, condemning those who cannot follow it perfectly. It required repeated sacrifices of animal blood. Conversely, the New Covenant is permanent, written on believers' hearts by the Holy Spirit, and based on grace through faith in Christ. His blood is the one-time everlasting sacrifice (2 Cor 3:7–18).

Paul then explains the paradox about glory and success (2 Cor 4–7): Society tends to place value on wealth, accomplishment, and worldly things, but God values humility, weakness, and suffering. Jesus suffered and died so our sins would be forgiven and we can be reconciled to God. This shows the value of Jesus's humility, sacrifice, and service, rather than self-promotion. Paul's ministry imitates Jesus and the cross, which means his life is the example of humility and suffering in the name of serving the Corinthians. Paul persists in order to transform the Corinthians.

Surrounding our passage, Paul reveals that he had an unbelievable spiritual event that couldn't be explained—a journey to the third heaven (spiritual realm of God's presence). God does not allow him to tell anyone about it nor does Paul reveal anything for fear that people may think too highly of him.[174] Visions were

_______________________

[174] John Christopher Thomas, "'An Angel from Satan': Paul's Thorn in the Flesh (2 Corinthians 12:7–10)," *Journal of Pentecostal Theology* 4, no. 9 (1996): 40.

common in the New Testament, and this was not Paul's only one (Acts 16:9–10; 18:9–11; 22:6–11; 26:12–20; 27:23–25). Even though Paul has good reason to brag, he humbly describes himself in the third person instead. Throughout Paul's ministry, he is not anxious to focus on himself, preferring to focus on Jesus. Paul does not speak of the holy and indescribable things he heard that God does not want others to know. He does not boast like the "super-apostles" would have foolishly done. He only boasts in the limitations that show his weakness, and if that makes him appear frail, he is happy to give God the glory. He shows that real strength comes from Christ, not from himself. Paul is joyful in his weakness because he is able to glorify God during his suffering.

Next, Paul transitions to the topic of the Corinthian's lack of generosity (2 Cor 8–9). In response to the poverty in Jerusalem, Paul wants the new churches to raise funds to symbolize unity in Jesus. The Corinthians had failed to save money for this cause, which shows that they have not been transformed by the gospel. Remember, Paul's mission is to spread the good news of Christ with the goal of transforming lives for Jesus, so the Corinthians' neglect to share in "this service to the Lord's people" (8:4, 9:1) is contrary to his objective.

Chapters 10–13 display Paul's humility as he boasts about his infirmities ("thorn in the flesh," trials, persecutions, and suffering) and his own knowledge about God. After all, he was raised as a Pharisee, a zealot, the most devout of all the Jews, who faithfully followed Jewish law before becoming a Christian. He now considers all the laws worthless compared to the exceeding value of knowing

Christ. His only desire is to encourage the Corinthian Christians in Jesus for their own well-being, not for any self-serving purposes. Paul ends his letter with a warning to the Corinthians (13) to test their own faithfulness and to live like followers of Jesus. He does not want to visit a third time to find them still unrepentant.

# Overall Meaning of the Passage

Second Corinthians 12:7–10 highlights the divine strength that comes from limitations. For Paul, his strength comes from his "thorn." What is this "thorn"? First, it is an infirmity that causes Paul a great deal of pain, irritation, and suffering; however, it does not appear to be life threatening.[175] It is characteristically evil since it causes Paul concern and pain, but it also serves a good purpose as a gift from God.[176] Whatever it is, Paul's thorn is most likely the cause of the Corinthians thinking less of him, and it keeps him humble, serving as a constant reminder that Paul can never be perfect in the flesh.

Since Paul does not disclose his specific struggle, it makes him a relatable modern-day messenger because this way no one is excluded from understanding his plight. Does Paul have one of my diseases? Is it the same "thorn" you have? Does it matter what his weakness is? The mystery of Paul's affliction brings a bigger blessing than if we are told his exact disability. Since we are left to

---

[175] Ibid., 43.
[176] Ralph P. Martin, *2 Corinthians* (Grand Rapids, MI: Zondervan Academic, 2014), Paul's Ecstasy.

wonder about the exact nature of Paul's suffering, we can fill in the blank with our own struggles. Like my own thorn, it appears that Paul's is visible. What "thorn" do you see in Paul? It is something that kept him humble and aware of his mortality despite the fact that he had experienced revelations worthy of bragging. It is a constant reminder that Paul needs to stay close to God.

Although Paul asks God to remove this weakness, God responds with "no." Paul's weakness is where Christ's power is displayed which is why he finds joy in his suffering (12:10)—because it is Christ working through him that strengthens him to do his work as an apostle; therefore, Paul sees the foolishness in boasting. Although the thorn is from God, Paul calls it a messenger of Satan that God allowed, just as He did with Job (Job 1–2). Rather than glorifying himself, Paul glories in his suffering and rejoices in his thorn. Does this sound familiar? Hint: Jesus's most vulnerable moment of suffering was when He hung on the cross. God then glorified Him by raising Him from the dead, and He saves all who believe in Him. God's grace is all we need. It transforms our weakness through God's strength and power. Paul never allows his thorn to make him bitter and angry or to question God's goodness. Instead, it causes him to grow and serve the Lord and "becomes the 'criterion of ministry.' From this account, Paul, with God's power on him, had turned weakness into victory."[177]

---

[177] Ibid.

# Discussion of Individual Verses

This passage is loaded with phrases that need further explanation. As we walk through these verses, God's message becomes very clear.

**2 Corinthians 12:7:** *"or because of these surpassingly great revelations. Therefore, in order to keep me from becoming conceited, I was given a thorn in my flesh, a messenger of Satan, to torment me."*

***"Or because of these surpassingly great revelations."*** These visions and revelations are from God, and they are so impressive that Paul could easily glorify himself for having this information, but he chooses to glorify God instead.

***"Therefore."*** Paul explains why he will not boast.

***"In order to keep me from becoming conceited."*** God does not want Paul to be conceited. If God showed me a secret, I would definitely be in danger of pride. In order to prevent Paul from becoming arrogant in his own abilities, God allows a "thorn" and "torment from Satan's messenger." "If the Corinthians wanted to place Paul on a pedestal, the thorn would prevent such action. . . . The emphasis is clear; Paul is weak, and this is further demonstrated by the thorn in the flesh."[178] James tells us that "God opposes the proud but shows favor to the humble" (Jas 4:6).

***"I was given."*** Paul is not responsible for his thorn; it was given to him—not thrust upon him but given like a gift. Paul views both the

---

[178] Ibid.

revelation and the thorn as gifts from God even though he wants this "thorn" removed. Although the thorn had some connection to Satan, it was given to prevent Paul from becoming prideful. Satan does not like humility, therefore, the thorn should be considered something God allowed for Paul's own good.[179]

***"A thorn."*** The Greek word for "thorn" is *skolops*. It is used to "denote something that frustrates and causes trouble in the lives of those afflicted."[180] *Skolops* suggests "the notion of something sharp and painful which sticks deeply in the flesh, and in the will of God defies extraction. The effect of its presence is to cripple Paul's enjoyment of life, and to frustrate his full efficiency by draining his energies."[181]

***"In my flesh."*** "Flesh" refers to Paul's actual body, not a theological concept. Scholars have offered a number of suggestions as to the nature of the thorn including "some physical or mental ailment, for example, eye trouble, attacks of malarial fever, stammering speech, epilepsy, headaches or a neurological disturbance. However, the plain fact is that there is insufficient data to decide the matter. Most modern interpreters prefer to see it as some sort of physical ailment, and the fact that Paul calls it a thorn in the flesh offers some support for this."[182]

***"A messenger of Satan."*** As we discussed earlier, God permits the thorn with Satan's assistance. This is reminiscent of when God

---

[179] Thomas, "'An Angel from Satan,'" 42–43.

[180] Colin G. Kruse, *2 Corinthians: An Introduction and Commentary* (Nottingham: IVP Academic, 2015), Commentary.

[181] Paul Barnett, *The Message of 2 Corinthians* (Westmont: InterVarsity Press, 2020), 164.

[182] Kruse, *2 Corinthians*, Paul Responds to a New Crisis.

allowed Satan to test Job (Job 1:6–22). God allows testing. Our suffering, like Paul's, imitates the suffering of Jesus (Col 1:24). This shows that evil is part of life on earth.[183]

***"To torment me."*** Different versions of the Bible use other words here like "batter," "buffet," or "hurt." All of these words indicate a persistent issue that would seem more like a physical ailment or a beating. Good things do not come to mind when we think of torment. It feels like something that will not end. I can relate to that. Can you?

**2 Corinthians 12:8:** *"Three times I pleaded with the Lord to take it away from me."*

***"Three times I pleaded with the Lord to take it away from me."*** Did Paul only pray three times? I doubt it. I pray every day for the removal of my "thorn." "Three times" may be a figure of speech here to represent his passionate desperation for relief. This is not just a casual request; Paul is pleading with God. Additionally, the number three signifies completeness in the Bible. Paul is doing what he had advised others to do in the face of trouble: "in every situation, by prayer and petition, with thanksgiving, present your requests to God" (Phil 4:6 NIV). Just like Jesus, Paul goes to God with his concerns, and as He did with Jesus, God denies Paul's request for the removal of his suffering. Paul does not turn to any vices to ease his suffering. (Okay, you caught me! Chocolate is my vice, but it is far better to turn to God. I'm working on that.) He is asking God to give him health and strength to replace the suffering and weakness, but

---

[183] Martin, *2 Corinthians*, Paul's Ecstasy.

sometimes God gives us transformation instead of removing the "thorn." Paul knows that God alone will take care of him and provide the lasting comfort that can be found nowhere else.

**2 Corinthians 12:9:** *"But he said to me, 'My grace is sufficient for you, for my power is made perfect in weakness.' Therefore I will boast all the more gladly about my weaknesses, so that Christ's power may rest on me."*

***"But he said to me, 'My grace is sufficient for you, for my power is made perfect in weakness.'"*** God answers Paul with this statement. It is not the answer Paul was hoping for, but the answer is for his benefit. God does not remove the thorn, but what Paul receives instead is much better: God's grace. Paul seems to be telling the Corinthians that God's answer provides comfort and strength. He is able to carry out God's work despite his "thorn." It is time for Paul to accept his situation, change his attitude, and submit to God's will. Ultimately, Satan will be overthrown, but he will run amuck here on earth in the meantime. At the same time, it is not necessarily God's will that His children have victory in this life whether through spiritual strength or physical recovery.[184] That's a big pill to swallow! God basically tells Paul that He will not remove Paul's "thorn," but by His grace, He will enable Paul to manage it. Then He adds "for my power is made perfect in weakness." Paul has God's grace and strength to overcome his obstacles, and God's grace never runs out. He is "the God of all grace" (1 Pet 5:10); we have the

---

[184] Barnett, *The Message of 2 Corinthians,* 164–65.

"word of his grace" (Acts 20:32); and we can approach His "throne of grace" (Heb 4:16) where we can receive His mercy in times of need.

Let's examine some key words more closely:

*Grace* is the assurance that there is no suffering that can conquer those who are in Christ (Rom 8:38–39). God provides what we cannot provide for ourselves. Grace transforms our hearts and our thinking.

*Sufficient* represents being enough; therefore, nothing can thwart Paul's service for God. God is sufficient, but we are insufficient. God's grace is all that Paul needs. It is enough.

*Power in weakness* is the power of Christ. God is certainly powerful enough to heal us, but He has a purpose for our pain. When we are weak, God's power becomes more obvious, but it is real whether it is obvious or not. This draws us closer to God. Acknowledging God's power is what makes Paul useful for the kingdom of God.

*Made perfect* signifies completion or fulfillment rather than flawlessness.

This verse is a reminder that God's strength is most evident when we are at our weakest, and His grace meets every need. God shows his strength through Paul's life—the strength does not come from Paul himself. All Paul needs to do, as do we, is rely on God's grace. We do not need to be flawless for God to use us. "God has more than compensated for the fact that the thorn was not removed."[185]

***"Therefore I will boast all the more gladly about my weaknesses."***
Here Paul responds to God's response. "In a way Paul has
experienced a cure, though not in the normal sense of the word. Paul
has received the power of Christ because he has accepted the answer
of God and proceeded to minister in spite of the thorn not being
removed."[186] Read that again. "Paul has experienced a cure." How
does that even make sense? Obviously, it is not a cure for our
suffering, but it can cure the attitude we have in our suffering. Paul's
gladness comes from boasting in his weaknesses instead of in
something else like "revelations and visions." The actual reading of
the text is "it is necessary to boast,"[187] meaning that Paul was
required to show the power of God. Most people would judge him as
weak and disgraceful, but Paul shows "the Corinthians an alternative
to the opponents that harass him. The alternative is strength-based-
on-weakness, a theme no doubt foreign to the opponents of Paul, but
one that expressed the heart of [Paul's] gospel of a crucified
Lord."[188] Paul still wants to show that he is not inferior to the "super-
apostles" (11:5; 12:11), but unlike his opponents, Paul points to
God's glory as he tries to get the Corinthians to see that the way of
the "super-apostles" is wrong.[189]

***"So that Christ's power may rest on me."*** Paul's secret to having
God's power "rest on him" is boasting about his weakness. This

---

[185] Martin, *2 Corinthians*, Paul's Ecstasy.
[186] Ibid.
[187] Ibid.
[188] Ibid.
[189] Ibid.

means "accepting God's will not to remove the thorn."[190] This is counterintuitive, as most people try to hide their flaws, but it is different in the kingdom of God where the only valuable thing to boast about is the power of Jesus. Since Christians are to be humble just as Jesus was humble, "thorns" are God's way of keeping His children humble whereas our pride gets in His way. While Paul is glad to brag about his weaknesses, he does not enjoy his difficulties; rather, he enjoys the power of Christ that rests upon him in these weaknesses. "The verb 'to rest upon' (*episkēnoō*) is quite rare. . . . It may, therefore, be better to translate the verb as 'dwell in' or 'reside.'"[191]

God's grace and power are combined to give Paul the strength he needs to minister to God's people. It is through Christ's power in us that God develops our character to be more like Christ. Paul, and we, must be completely dependent on God.


**2 Corinthians 12:10:** *"That is why, for Christ's sake, I delight in weaknesses, in insults, in hardships, in persecutions, in difficulties. For when I am weak, then I am strong."*

***"That is why, for Christ's sake, I delight in weaknesses, in insults, in hardships, in persecutions, in difficulties."*** Paul accepts his disability as he becomes conscious of Christ's power.[192] It is "in the pain of suffering of both body and mind that the same grace pins us closer to Christ, who says to us, 'my power is made perfect in

---

[190] Ibid.

[191] Kruse, *2 Corinthians*, Paul Responds to a New Crisis.

[192] Martin, *2 Corinthians*, Paul's Ecstasy.

weakness.'"[193] Paul identifies his weakness Christologically. In other words, what he is suffering is for Christ. Paul recognizes Christ as weak in the crucifixion, but then he sees God's power in the resurrection. God's power is completed in Jesus's suffering. Paul's weakness is the "best possible hope for the display of divine power."[194] Does that make sense? We have the opportunity to display God's power when we accept our thorns. This is part of God's plan.

"The verb translated *delight in* (*eudokeō*) may also be translated 'be content with' (NRSV)."[195] It's not that Paul enjoys his suffering, but he can find joy and contentment despite his suffering because he knows that the power of Christ will be with him in the midst of his trials. Since Paul's opponents belittle his claims to be an apostle because of his weakness, he explains how divine power shows up in human weakness, supporting his own claim to be an apostle while denying the claims of those who disagree with him.[196] Paul's love for Christ is so deep-rooted that his willingness to suffer surpasses his desire to be healed. Can you say that? If our love for Christ is number one, then nothing else matters. This is why Paul delights for Christ's sake. Christ has overcome the world (John 16:33), including suffering. Through Paul's acceptance and handling of his suffering, he is glorifying Christ.

***"For when I am weak, then I am strong."*** God does not allow Paul's suffering to keep him down. Paul withstands not just this

---

[193] Barnett, *The Message of 2 Corinthians*, 167.
[194] Martin, *2 Corinthians*, Paul's Ecstasy.
[195] Kruse, *2 Corinthians*, Paul Responds to a New Crisis.
[196] Ibid.

"thorn" but also imprisonment, shipwreck, and persecution. Through this, he is able to establish churches, train others, and preach to many. He is only able to do this through God's grace and strength. This is why he is able to say, "I can do all things through Christ who strengthens me" (Phil 4:13). Ultimately, Paul welcomes his "thorn" and the opportunity to rely on God.

# Theological Reflections

"Paul's letters to the church of Corinth are among the most theologically rich and most practically helpful books in the [New Testament]."[197] As he responds to the many church-related issues, Paul exhibits his unwavering faith along with his need to keep up with daily challenges. He puts his faith into practice.

Paul addresses numerous theological themes in his writing. He presents the many roles of God: "God and Father of our Lord Jesus Christ" (1:3; 11:31); "the Father of compassion" (1:3); and "the God of all comfort" (1:3, 7:6). Paul also describes what God does: He raises the dead (1:9); He makes "his light shine in our hearts to give us the light of the knowledge of God's glory displayed in the face of Christ" (4:6); He causes the believer to "stand firm in Christ. He anoints us, sets his seal of ownership on us, and puts his Spirit in our hearts as a deposit, guaranteeing what is to come [salvation]" (1:21–22, 5:5); He "leads us as captives in Christ's triumphal procession and uses us to spread the aroma of the knowledge of

---

[197] Köstenberger, Kellum, and Quarles, *The Lion and the Lamb*, 177.

[Christ]" (2:14); and He makes us "competent as ministers of a new covenant" (3:6). He makes us a "new creation" (5:17); He "reconciled us to himself through Christ and gave us the ministry of reconciliation…not counting people's sins against them" (5:18–19); He makes us "Christ's ambassadors" (5:20); He "comforts the downcast" (7:6); He blesses us "abundantly" (9:8); and most importantly, He gives us "his indescribable gift [Jesus]" (9:15).[198] Primary to Paul's theology is God's promise of the New Covenant in Jesus as prophesied (Jer 31:31–34; Ezek 36:24–30) and its superiority over the old covenant, which results in death.[199]

Our passage places human suffering on a theological level. Verses 9–10 introduce the Christological theme and a defense for Paul's service for Christ. Paul's suffering is then seen within the framework of God's grace. This grace not only permits Paul's ailment but also sustains him in his suffering.[200] God provides comfort in suffering, strength in weakness, life through death, and blessing in suffering.

## Pointing to Jesus

While Paul speaks of the many attributes of God, his message centers around Jesus Christ. Paul's description of Jesus reminds us of who He is:

> The Son of God (1:19), the image of God (4:4) and the one in whose face the glory of God is displayed (4:6). He refers to

---

198 Kruse, *2 Corinthians*, Theology and Major Themes.
199 Köstenberger, Kellum, and Quarles, *The Lion and the Lamb*, 204–5.
200 Martin, *2 Corinthians*, Paul's Ecstasy.

Christ's humility and gentleness (10:1) and his generosity in becoming "poor" so that believers might become "rich" (8:9). He speaks of Christ authoring a "letter" of recommendation for his ministry, a letter inscribed with the Spirit in human hearts through the apostle's own ministry (3:3). He says the life of Jesus is revealed in his body (4:10–11), that the power of Christ rests on him, making him strong despite his weakness (12:9–10), that the love of Christ compels him (5:14) and that Christ speaks through him (13:3). He teaches that God was in Christ reconciling the world to himself (5:19), that because Christ has died for all, God regards them all as having died (5:14), and that all must appear before the judgment seat of Christ to receive recompense for what they have done "while in the body" (5:10).[201]

Paul's themes include discussions on the resurrection of Christ and the resurrected body of believers (1 Cor 15). He reminds the Corinthians that Jesus's death had been prophesied in Old Testament Scripture, and that without this belief, our faith is useless. Jesus was the first to be resurrected, and believers will follow, so Paul speaks of the glory that is still to come. In the meantime, our hardships and suffering bring us closer to the grace of Christ. This is the main point of Paul's boasting.[202] Paul encourages believers not to lose heart in their suffering when he says, "Though outwardly we are wasting away, yet inwardly we are being renewed day by day. For our light and momentary troubles are achieving for us an eternal glory that far outweighs them all" (4:16–17). Our suffering does not feel like "light and momentary troubles," but Paul is in it for the long haul, knowing "that the one who raised the Lord Jesus from the dead

---

[201] Kruse, *2 Corinthians*, Theology and Major Themes.
[202] Martin, *2 Corinthians*, Paul's Ecstasy.

will also raise us with Jesus" (4:14). Because of Jesus's sacrifice, we will be free of our suffering upon His return, at which time we will have new bodies relieved of pain (5:1–5). How amazing!

# Application

For Paul to be faithful in his ministry in spite of his "thorn" was a massive responsibility and could not have been easy. I would imagine that he had days of total frustration. Paul's story demonstrates the Christian principle that suffering can transform lives. His acceptance of his weakness reminds us that our faith is strengthened through our suffering, a truth Jesus lived as well. Second Corinthians 12:7–10 specifically provides comfort and encouragement in the face of suffering. Pain changes our perspective. As we accept our "thorns," we can let go of the need to be "perfect" or "normal" and live a more authentic life. I have always tried to appear as close to "normal" as possible, but that has caused me nothing but emotional pain on top of the physical weakness. It is just not worth it, nor is it godly. This is how God created me. Acceptance is the key. When I shift my focus off of me and back to Him, I am better able to serve Him with a joyful heart.

To apply the message of our passage, we must first acknowledge that we have a "thorn." We need to be honest with ourselves, God, and others. Paul shared his trials with others, and we can too. Praying for strength and surrendering our suffering to God brings us closer to Him. He is our loving Father who wants to help us. As we accept our challenges and rely on God, we have Christ's power in us to handle suffering with faith and confidence. Can you be joyful in the midst of your suffering? I am not saying that this is easy, but the solution is plain. Trust that Christ's power is made perfect in our weakness (12:9). God wants us to rest in His strength. If God wants to deliver us from our suffering, He can do that. If not, He gives us the power and grace to carry on. I don't know about you, but I would love to be independent and self-sufficient. I do not like to burden others. Maybe this is prideful. I have had to learn to accept help—even simple things like opening a water bottle or chopping food. This definitely keeps me humble! My thorns have taken away my arrogance.

God allows suffering in our lives, but it is our choice how we deal with it. We can be angry and blame God; we can just give up; we can grin and bear it; or we can use it for His glory. When we recognize that God is all we need, we realize that God will take care of us regardless of our circumstances. He did it for Paul, and He will do it for you and me too. Like Paul, we can glory in our suffering by finding joy in our hardships, strengthening our faith, and deepening our relationship with God, knowing that Christ dwells in us and we are doing God's work. Our thorns keep us humble. I can attest to that. My "thorn" is what brought me to author this book. Without my diseases and consequent suffering, I would have nothing to write about. I would have no testimony, and God's power would not be displayed. He chose my weakness to show His strength. It amazes me when I stop to think about it. I have to admit that there are many days when I feel like I am under attack by Satan, but God sustains me. He gives me the strength to endure through my weaknesses. If we fight against our "thorns" instead of accepting them as gifts from God, they will be a curse to us and others instead of being the blessing that God intends them to be.

Be confident of this: He will carry us through the suffering (Heb 4:16). When we stop trying to control or fix our weaknesses, that is when God's strength works best. Paradoxically, we need to be weak to be strong. It sounds crazy, but it's true. As we remain faithful to God, He works through us. As others see God's work in us, He is glorified. If we do not turn to God, our "thorns" can become a true curse. We need faith and God's grace to turn our "thorns" into blessings. One way to do this is to make a list of God's grace toward us. Let me get you started:

- By God's grace you were born.
- By God's grace you are saved.
- By God's grace you have many blessings.
  Name them.
- By God's grace you have faith.
- By God's grace you can endure your suffering.

Now it's your turn. As you make your list, remember that Paul's situation teaches us valuable lessons: (1) spiritual restoration is more important than physical healing; (2) God balances our suffering with His glory; (3) sometimes God allows Satan to "torment" us to achieve His purposes; (4) pride is worse than suffering; (5) do not allow your "thorn" to prevent you from serving God; and (6) trust God. "True ministry in Christ's name involves both suffering and victory."[203]

Some people will be delivered from their suffering in this life, but in His sovereignty, God does not heal all of us. Why? Because He has a plan for you and me that serves His divine purpose, and our "thorn" is a crucial part of His design. It is natural to ask for healing, but maybe instead of praying for escape from our suffering, we need to pray for our pain to transform us. Without your suffering, can you be useful for the kingdom of God? Would you have the same power without your pain? The answer is no; otherwise, your suffering would not exist. It is in our acceptance of our "thorns" that we embrace humility. Pray and trust. Our spiritual state will always be more important than our physical disabilities (or whatever challenges you're facing). It is time for you and me to adjust our thinking and view our suffering as the blessing God intended. Paul tells us to be "confident and know that as long as we are at home in the body we are away from the Lord" (5:6). We are to be "be strong in the Lord and in his mighty power" (Eph 6:10). As we live in God's strength, we bring glory to His name, even in our weakness. Are you strong enough to embrace your weakness and therefore be strong in Christ?

---

[203] R. E. Glaze, and Chad Brand, "Second Letter to the Corinthians" in Brand, *Holman Illustrated Bible Dictionary*, 349.

## Literary and Historical Context

**Author:** Second Corinthians was written by Paul the apostle through divine inspiration. While he was known as an exceptional leader (2 Cor 12:12), Paul was a "timid" speaker (10:1), his physical presence was unimpressive (2 Cor 10:10), and he was not the picture of health (2 Cor 12:7; Gal 4:13–14).

**Date:** The book of Acts provides some reference points to help determine that Paul wrote 2 Corinthians in AD 56. On Paul's first visit to Corinth he found Aquila and his wife Priscilla, Jews who had just arrived from Italy because Emperor Claudius had ordered the Jews to leave Rome in AD 49 (Acts 18:2). Next, Acts 18:12–17 tells us that Paul was brought before Gallio, the proconsul of Achaia, during his first visit to Corinth. Archaeological evidence hints that Gallio was in office in Corinth from the spring of AD 51 to the spring of AD 52, but he did not finish his term, so Paul most likely met Gallio in the summer of AD 51. Given these points of reference, a timeline for Paul's connections with the Corinthians can be derived. Paul's first visit to Corinth started in early AD 50. After eighteen months, he was arraigned before Gallio (second half of AD 51), after which he stayed in Corinth "for some time" (Acts 18:18), then he sailed to Antioch. He spent "some time" there, "then traveled from place to place throughout the region of Galatia and Phrygia" (Acts 18:23) for two years and three months (AD 52–55). Scholars agree that he wrote 1 Corinthians in AD 55 in response to reports of issues in the church. Paul continued his ministry in Ephesus, which was so successful that "all the Jews and Greeks who lived in the province of Asia heard the word of the Lord" (Acts 19:10). However, the Corinthians continued their hostile assaults on Paul. After a "painful visit" to Corinth, Paul determined not to return (2 Cor 2:1). While Paul was in Macedonia, his spiritual son Titus brought him good news of improvement in Corinth in response to Paul's letter of rebuke,[204] so he wrote 2 Corinthians 1-9 in AD 56, expressing his joy over their repentance and promising to visit again[205] (2 Cor 7:5; 8:1; 9:2); but their attitude declined again, so Paul then penned chapters 10–13 to correct their arrogance and to defend his apostolic authority.[206]

**Audience**: Paul wrote to "God's church at Corinth" (2 Cor 1:1). He intended the letter to be read by many congregations, specifically those in Achaia. At that time, the population was probably about 200,000; however, some scholars and ancient writers speculated that it was much more sizable. This would indicate that Corinth was eight times larger than the major city of Athens.[207]

**Historical Time and Background:** Corinth was the leading commercial center of southern Greece in the first century due to its advantageous location on the isthmus connecting northern

---

[204] Glaze and Brand, "Second Letter to the Corinthians," 348.

[205] Colin G. Kruse, Andreas J. Köstenberger, and Robert W. Yarbrough, *2 Corinthians* (Nashville, TN: B&H Academic, 2020), Date and Provenance.

[206] Köstenberger, Kellum, and Quarles, *The Lion and the Lamb*, 180.

[207] Ibid.

Greece with the Peloponnesus. With two harbors and numerous roads, Corinth became a popular stop for ships carrying merchandise, especially pottery and bronze, which were exported throughout the Mediterranean for a century (ca. 350–250 BC).[208] The city became well-known internationally and housed a racially mixed population, resulting in a diversification of religious cults. Since they were near the site of the Isthmian games (ancient Greek competitions) that were held every two years, the Corinthians were able to enjoy the games as well as the wealth brought by visitors to the city.[209] Corinth became known in the ancient world as a wealthy and immoral city to the extent that the term "corinthianize" meant to fornicate.

After starting his ministry in the synagogue where he tried to "persuade Jews and Greeks" (Acts 18:4), Paul formed a church in the house of Titius Justus, a converted newcomer to the religion, which attracted members from the pagan world through his preaching. "The Lord spoke to Paul in a vision" (Acts 18:9–10), and Paul established a Christian community even though Jews tried to bring the civil authority against him (Acts 18:4–18).[210]

About two hundred years before Paul's visit, the Roman conqueror L. Mummius had destroyed the city. About a century after the destruction, Julius Caesar reconstructed Corinth (46–44

---

[208] R. E. Glaze and Chad Brand, "Corinth" in Brand, *Holman Illustrated Bible Dictionary*, 344.
[209] Ibid., 345.
[210] Martin, *2 Corinthians*, ch. 1.

BC) as a Roman colony.[211] Corinth's commercial favorability had already been established before Paul's arrival.

**Geographic Context:** Since the Corinthians controlled both the east-west trade across the isthmus and the trade between Peloponnesus and the area of Greece to the north,[212] Paul was able to use the sea traffic between Ephesus and Corinth to communicate with his church.[213]

**Religions of Corinth:** While the rebuilt city of Corinth was a Roman city, its citizens still worshiped Greek gods. On one side of the city stood the old temple of Apollo with a shrine to Apollo as well as shrines to Hermes, Hercules, Athena, and Poseidon. There was a temple dedicated to Asclepius, the god of healing, and his daughter Hygieia. The cult of Aphrodite was the most significant. Aphrodite worship had been popular before the city's destruction in 146 BC and was renewed in Roman Corinth with Aphrodite's temple located on the top of the Acropolis.[214] The city included a Jewish community as well.

**Literary Background:** This text has been the subject of much debate. The main issue revolves around the literary integrity of the letter, with many scholars questioning whether chapters 10–13 are original to the letter.[215] The surviving ancient copies of 2 Corinthians all have the letter as a single piece of work, but the Bible itself suggests that Paul most likely wrote separate letters in

---

[211] Ibid.

[212] Glaze and Brand, "Corinth," 344.

[213] Burge and Green, *The New Testament in Antiquity*, 388.

[214] Glaze and Brand, "Corinth," 344–345.

[215] Thomas, "'An Angel from Satan,'" 43.

stages over time. This could explain some of the disconnections in the document identified by scholars, but this was not a customary practice.[216] The letter seems to break with chapter 10, which begins a different style and theme. Chapters 1–9 have a confident tone, but Paul's tone changes in chapter 10 "as he launches into a violent and sarcastic attack with his apostolic standing again, a subject of heated debate. Paul is clearly on the defensive."[217] Some say that the current arrangement of 2 Corinthains was done by an editor who pulled the pieces together as a whole to represent Paul's last will and testament to the churches.[218] Other options include the idea that the letter was written in order describing a sequential pattern; that chapters 10–13 were written by Paul later;[219] or that as a very emotional and personal letter, it could have been written as if the Corinthians were present with Paul.[220]

**Structure and Organization:** The book is divided into three parts: Paul's peacemaking with the Corinthian church (1–7), generosity in the Jerusalem church (8–9), and challenging those who reject Paul (10–13). The literary plan shows Paul handling criticism from his opponents, especially regarding his boasting even though he is only boasting about his own weakness. Paul wants to show that his ministry, not that of the false apostles, is the one of God.[221] Paul uses judicial rhetoric to defend himself as

---

[216] Burge and Green, *The New Testament in Antiquity*, 391.
[217] Martin, *2 Corinthians*, ch. 6.
[218] Ibid.
[219] Ibid..
[220] Burge and Green, *The New Testament in Antiquity*, 393.
[221] Martin, *2 Corinthians*, Paul's Ecstasy and Its Evaluation.

an apostle and encourages his audience to make well-informed decisions about the false "super-apostles."[222]

Many scholars have struggled to classify the book without any particular analysis winning, so most critics prefer to analyze the structure of the letter based strictly on content.[223]

The major themes in 2 Corinthians are Paul's transparency about the nature and authority of true ministry; his petitions to the Corinthians to contribute to the financial needs of Christians in Jerusalem just as the churches in Macedonia and Asia were doing; his comparison between the old and new covenants; and his discussion on the state of the body between death and resurrection.[224]

**Genre and Literary Style:** Second Corinthians qualifies as an ancient Greco-Roman letter, known as an epistle, but it is different in that it was addressed to a Christian community rather than to an individual. Second Corinthians follows the general framework of ancient letters: an opening greeting (1:1–2), a thanksgiving segment (1:3), the body of the letter (1:4–13:10), and a farewell (13:11–14). It veers from the traditional format in that Paul blesses God not for His grace but rather for the comfort He provides in the middle of suffering. Paul provides the hope for his audience that by sharing in suffering, they will share in comfort too just as he has.[225] Although different than the typical blessing, it accomplishes the characteristic bond with the

---

[222] Kruse, *2 Corinthians*, Intro: Literary Matters.
[223] Köstenberger, Kellum, and Quarles, *The Lion and the Lamb*, 188.
[224] Glaze and Brand, "Second Letter to the Corinthians," 348.
[225] Kruse, *2 Corinthians*, Analysis.

audience.

**Biblical Context:** Because the early church fathers accepted the letter as authentic, it was included in the canon.[226] There are references to the book as early as the end of the first century AD. It is listed in the Muratorian Canon (one of the oldest lists of the books recognized as Scripture) in AD 170 as well as in heretical early scriptures (AD 140). Additionally, it appears in the second-century early Greek New Testament manuscript written on papyrus known as $P^{46}$. In the late second century and into the third century, it is quoted by early Christian theologians.[227]

The book contributes to the canon in its discussion of the redemptive grace of suffering, the revelation of God's power, and the reality of human weakness (2 Cor 1:3–11; 4:7–18; 12:1–10). It brings understanding to the new covenant and helps build the theology of suffering unlike any other New Testament book. Equally important, the Corinthian letters, notably 2 Corinthians, help develop a biblical understanding of faith that accentuates compassion, sacrifice, humility, and reliance on God. Today, some pastors achieve rock-star status in mega-churches while humility is underrated, making 2 Corinthians just as relevant today as it was in the time of Paul.[228]

---

[226] Burge and Green, *The New Testament in Antiquity,* 390.
[227] Ibid., 390.
[228] Köstenberger, Kellum, and Quarles, *The Lion and the Lamb*, 178.

Chapter 7

# WHAT DOES IT ALL MEAN?

## Conclusion

If you are reading this book, please know that I am praying for you. It is my prayer that these chapters have encouraged you to trust God with your circumstances. The Bible is full of Scripture showing that our suffering has a purpose. I hope this gets you started.

The most important aspect of being in relationship with God is just loving Him and abiding in His presence. Knowing God is more valuable than knowing all the answers. Read that again. We do not need to have all the answers. In other words, we do not need to know why we suffer. We just need to know that God is in control. Life does not always make sense from our human perspective. It is especially in those moments when despair is ruling our lives when God calls us to turn to Him and trust Him wholeheartedly. God is good. . . . always. His love for us does not waver. It is the challenges that make us stronger. Remember, God loves us so much that He sent His Son to die for our sins. You and I are valuable to God. Whatever we are suffering through does not change who God is or how He views us. Rather, suffering strengthens our faith because it helps us relate to Christ and His suffering, enables us to see God's hand at work in our lives, and provides us with the words we need to support others on their journey.

Everything we endure here on earth is preparing us for eternity, so persevere and keep a grateful heart. When Jesus returns or calls us home, all suffering will end. The Bible promises that "He will wipe every tear from [our] eyes. There will be no more death or mourning or crying or pain, for the old order of things has passed away" (Rev 21:4 NIV). Our story has a beautiful and pain-free ending. We will suffer no more. That is the promise of God.

# *Appendix A*

## CHARCOT-MARIE-TOOTH DISEASE

**What is Charcot-Marie-Tooth Disease (CMT)?**
Charcot-Marie-Tooth disease (CMT) is one of the most common inherited neurological conditions, impacting about 1 in 2,500 people worldwide. It affects the peripheral nerves, those outside the brain and spinal cord, which control movement and sensation in the limbs.

**What Does CMT Do?**
CMT causes the nerves that activate muscles and transmit sensory signals to slowly degenerate. Over time, this leads to:
- Muscle weakness and atrophy in the hands, feet, arms, and legs
- Foot deformities (high arches, hammertoes)
- Poor balance and frequent tripping or falling
- Numbness, tingling, or burning in the limbs
- Chronic fatigue and nerve pain
- Difficulty with fine motor skills (e.g., writing, buttoning a shirt)

Symptoms typically begin in adolescence or early adulthood but can appear at any age. The severity and progression vary widely, even within the same family.

**Daily Life with CMT**
Living with CMT often means adapting to a body that doesn't always cooperate. Walking long distances, climbing stairs, or standing for extended periods can be difficult or exhausting. Many people with CMT wear leg braces (AFOs) for stability and mobility. Others may rely on canes, walkers, or wheelchairs, especially as symptoms progress.
Simple tasks like tying shoes, opening jars, or keeping up with peers in physical activities may require extra time or support. Still, with the right tools and care, people with CMT lead full, meaningful lives, often becoming experts at finding creative ways to navigate their world.

**Is There a Cure?**
There is currently no cure for CMT, but treatment options such as physical and occupational therapy, bracing, pain management, and surgical interventions can help manage symptoms. Research is ongoing, and promising therapies are on the horizon.

**Want to Learn More?**
Visit the Charcot-Marie-Tooth Association (CMTA) at www.cmtausa.org

With permission of the Charcot-Marie-Tooth Association

# *Appendix B*

## SJOGREN'S DISEASE

Sjögren's disease is a serious and systemic autoimmune disease that presents with symptoms of extensive dryness (eyes, mouth, skin), profound fatigue, and chronic pain. Other serious manifestations can include major organ involvement (e.g., kidney, lung, heart, pancreas); neurological symptoms (peripheral neuropathy, dysautonomia, migraines, aseptic meningitis); and lymphoma.

People with Sjögren's disease are 44 times more likely to develop lymphoma than those who do not have Sjögren's disease.

Sjögren's is the 2nd most common rheumatic autoimmune disease in the United States. Affecting as many as four million Americans, Sjögren's is three times more common than better known related diseases such as lupus and multiple sclerosis.

Ninety percent (90%) of adults diagnosed with Sjögren's are women, and 10% are men. In pediatric cases, the female predominance is less skewed. Historically, Sjögren's has been considered a disease of older women, contributing to delays in diagnosis for men, children, and younger women. The disease has been recognized across nearly all racial and ethnic groups.

Diagnosing Sjögren's is difficult and can often take years for a person to receive an accurate diagnosis. This is because the disease presents differently in people living with Sjögren's, with a wide range of symptoms that can mimic other conditions and diseases. The disease has also been misunderstood and misrepresented as only a dry mouth and dry eye disease that affects older women. Proper awareness is essential for accurate diagnosis and treatment.

There is no specific treatment for Sjögren's although healthcare providers often prescribe immune modulating drugs (such as hydroxychloroquine) or immune suppressants (such as methotrexate or rituximab). Healthcare providers also prescribe anti-inflammatory eyedrops, such as cyclosporine, to reduce ocular inflammation to control dryness. Over-the-counter products, such as eyedrops and oral moisture aids, are used for comfort.

There is no known cure for Sjögren's.

**Sjögren's ("SHOW-grins") is a systemic autoimmune disease that affects the entire body.**

- Neurological problems, concentration/ memory-loss, dysautonomia, headaches

- Dry eyes, corneal ulcerations and infections

- Dry nose, recurrent sinusitis, nose bleeds

- Dry mouth, mouth sores, dental decay, difficulty with chewing, speech, taste and dentures

- Swollen, painful parotid/ salivary glands

- Difficulty swallowing, heartburn, reflux, esophagitis

- Fatigue, vasculitis, lymphoma, dry skin

- Recurrent bronchitis, interstitial lung disease, pneumonia

- Arthritis, muscle pain

- Abnormal liver function tests, chronic active autoimmune hepatitis, primary biliary cholangitis

- Interstitial nephritis, renal tubular acidosis, glomerulonephritis

- Peripheral neuropathy, Raynaud's

- Stomach upset, gastroparesis, autoimmune pancreatitis

- Irritable bowel, autoimmune gastrointestinal dysmotility

- Interstitial cystitis

- Vaginal dryness, vulvodynia (women only); chronic prostatitis (men only)

LEARN MORE Sjögrens.org     info@sjogrens.org
With permission of the Sjogren's Foundation. Sjogrens.org

# *Appendix C*

## EHLERS-DANLOS DISEASE

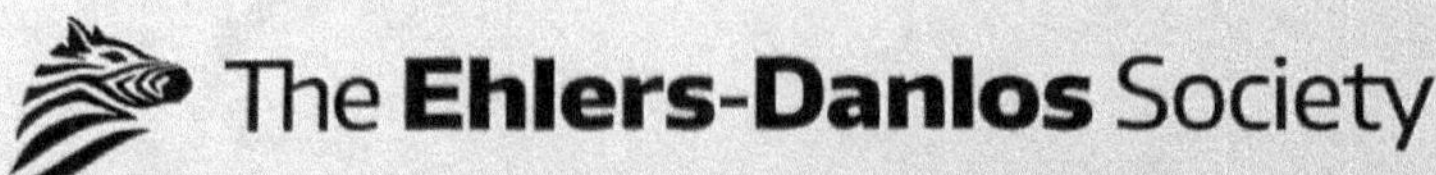


### What are the Ehlers-Danlos syndromes?

The Ehlers-Danlos syndromes (EDS) are a group of connective tissue disorders that can be inherited and are varied, both in how they affect the body and in their genetic causes. They are generally characterized by joint hypermobility (joints that stretch further than normal), skin hyperextensibility (skin that can be stretched further than normal), and tissue fragility.

Connective tissue is the material in the body that binds together, supports, and separates different tissues and organs. Found between other tissues everywhere in the body, it provides strength and flexibility, and helps perform general functions as well as specialized services. Connective tissue disorders disrupt these most fundamental processes and structures of the body, so resulting problems can be widespread, in a wide range of severities, and affect areas that might seem to be otherwise unrelated.

**Early diagnosis is crucial to positive patient health**. Symptoms can be treated as they arise. Care is largely preventative, to support and manage EDS with the intent of keeping damage as minimal as possible. Specifics have to be tailored to those symptoms exhibited in the person with EDS. EDS is known to affect people of all ages, races, and genders.

EDS are currently classified into thirteen subtypes. A person's physical signs and symptoms will be matched up to the major and minor criteria to identify the subtype that is the most complete fit. There is substantial symptom overlap between EDS and other connective tissue disorders, so a definitive diagnosis for EDS when the gene mutation is known—all but hypermobile EDS—also calls for confirmation by testing to identify the responsible variant for the gene affected.

Please remember that an individual's experience with an EDS is their own, and may not necessarily be the same as another person's experience. Diagnostic criteria are meant solely to distinguish an EDS from other connective tissue disorders, and there are many more possible symptoms for each EDS than there are criteria.

**Classical** [COL5A1, COL5A2, rarely COL1A1]
**Classical-like** [TNXB]
**Cardiac-valvular** [COL1A2]
**Vascular** [COL3A1, rarely COL1A1]: possibility of shortened lifespan; arterial rupture is the most common cause of sudden death.
**Hypermobile** [no identified cause]
**Arthrochalasia** [COL1A1, COL1A2]
**Dermatosparaxis** [ADAMTS2]
**Kyphoscoliotic** [PLOD1, FKBP14]
**Brittle cornea syndrome** [ZNF469, PRDM5]
**Spondylodysplastic** [B4GALT7, B3GALT6, SLC39A13]
**Musculocontractural** [CHST14, DSE]
**Myopathic** [COL12A1]
**Periodontal** [C1R, C1S]

# For more information, **ehlers-danlos.com**

With permission of the Ehlers-Danlos Society

# Appendix D

# DYSAUTONOMIA

**Dysautonomia** (dis-auto-NO-mia) is a term used to describe any disorder of the autonomic nervous system. The **autonomic nervous system (ANS)** is the part of the nervous system that regulates functions that are automatic in nature such as heart rate, blood pressure, digestion, excretion, perspiration, temperature regulation, pupil dilation, circulation, and respiration among others. The ANS is responsible for maintaining homeostasis, or equilibrium, in the body. When there is a dysfunction or failure of the autonomic nervous system, the result is a disorder classified as a type of dysautonomia, an umbrella term to describe autonomic disorders. It's also referred to as autonomic dysfunction or autonomic neuropathy. Often dysautonomias are invisible illnesses. Patients may not look sick, and yet they have symptoms that make it difficult to perform activities of daily living.

**Common symptoms:**
- Difficulty Standing Still
- Fatigue
- Lightheadedness
- Nausea and Other GI Symptoms
- Brain Fog and Mental Clouding
- Palpitations or Chest Discomfort
- Shortness of Breath or Difficulty Breathing

Dysautonomia symptoms are not limited to these seven. The organ systems most commonly affected in dysautonomias are neurological, pulmonary, cardiovascular, urinary, gastrointestinal, secretomotor and pupillomotor. Because autonomic disorders affect multiple organ systems, the presentation of symptoms are heterogenous, widely varying between different individuals.

Pupillomotor Symptoms: impaired pupil response and impaired vision.

Neurological Symptoms: migraines, cognitive deficits, brain fog and mental clouding.

Pulmonary Symptoms: shortness of breath, easily winded, and difficulty breathing.

Cardiovascular Symptoms: palpitations, chest discomfort, high heart rate (tachycardia), low heart rate (bradycardia), high or low blood pressure, abnormal blood pressure functioning, and blood pooling.

Urinary Symptoms: difficulty with urine retention and/or excretion.

Gastrointestinal Symptoms: nausea, vomiting, diarrhea, constipation, abdominal pain, reflux, heartburn, and impaired motility

Secretomotor Symptoms: difficulty sweating, tearing, and other fluid production (dry eyes, dry mouth, difficulty swallowing, dry skin).

Orthostatic Intolerance Symptoms: difficulty standing still, fatigue, lightheadedness, increase in symptoms with upright posture, fainting (syncope) or near-fainting, and pallor.

https://thedysautonomiaproject.org/dysautonomia/

# Bible Abbreviations

## Old Testament

| | | | |
|---|---|---|---|
| Gen | Genesis | Dan | Daniel |
| Exod | Exodus | Hos | Hosea |
| Lev | Leviticus | Joel | Joel |
| Num | Numbers | Amos | Amos |
| Deut | Deuteronomy | Obad | Obadiah |
| Josh | Joshua | Jonah | Jonah |
| Judg | Judges | Mic | Micah |
| Ruth | Ruth | Nah | Nahum |
| 1&2 Sam | 1&2 Samuel | Hab | Habakkuk |
| 1&2 Kgs | 1&2 Kings | Zeph | Zephaniah |
| 1&2 Chron | 1&2 Chronicles | Hag | Haggai |
| Ezra | Ezra | Zech | Zechariah |
| Neh | Nehemiah | Mal | Malachi |
| Esth | Esther | | |
| Job | Job | | |
| Ps/Pss | Psalm/Psalms | | |
| Prov | Proverbs | | |
| Eccl | Ecclesiastes | | |
| Song | Song of Solomon | | |
| Isa | Isaiah | | |
| Jer | Jeremiah | | |
| Lam | Lamentations | | |
| Ezek | Ezekiel | | |

| | |
|---|---|
| Matt | Matthew |
| Mark | Mark |
| Luke | Luke |
| John | John |
| Acts | Acts |
| Rom | Romans |
| 1&2 Cor | 1&2 Corinthians |
| Gal | Galatians |
| Eph | Ephesians |
| Phil | Philippians |
| Col | Colossians |
| 1&2 Thess | 1&2 Thessalonians |
| 1&2 Tim | 1&2 Timothy |
| Titus | Titus |
| Phlm | Philemon |
| Heb | Hebrews |
| Jas | James |
| 1&2 Pet | 1&2 Peter |
| 1, 2, 3 John | 1, 2, 3 John |
| Jude | Jude |
| Rev | Revelation |

<u>**Bible Versions**</u>

| | |
|---|---|
| ESV | English Standard Version |
| MSG | The Message |
| NIV | New International Version |
| NRSV | New Revised Standard Version |
| RSV | Revised Standard Version |

# Bibliography


Allison, Dale C., Jr. *James: A Critical and Exegetical Commentary.* International Critical Commentary. London: Bloomsbury, 2013.

Bang, Ki-Min. "A Missing Key to Understanding Psalm 46: Revisiting the Chaoskampf." *Conversations with the Biblical World* 37 (2017): 68–89.

Barnett, Paul. *The Message of 2 Corinthians.* Westmont: InterVarsity Press, 2020.

Bartholomew, Craig G., and Ryan P. O'Dowd. *Old Testament Wisdom Literature: A Theological Introduction.* Westmont: InterVarsity Press, 2011.

Blomberg, Craig L., and Mariam J. Kovalishyn. *James.* Grand Rapids, MI: Zondervan Academic, 2008.

Brand, Chad, ed. *Holman Illustrated Bible Dictionary.* Nashville, TN: B&H, 2015.

Brandell, Eric. "Discerning the Literary Structure in the Epistle of James." *Stone-Campbell Journal* 25, no. 2 (2022): 229–39.

Bray, Gerald L., and Thomas C. Oden, eds. *James, 1-2 Peter, 1-3 John, Jude.* Westmont: InterVarsity Press, 2000.

Brooks, James A. *Mark: An Exegetical and Theological Exposition of Holy Scripture.* Nashville: B&H, 1991.

Burge, Gary M., and Gene L. Green, *The New Testament in Antiquity*. 2nd ed. Grand Rapids, MI: Zondervan Academic, 2020.

Caulley, Thomas Scott. "The Place of Abba in Mark's Christology." *Bulletin for Biblical Research* 32, no. 4 (2022): 394–416.

Donahue, John R., and Daniel J. Harrington, Sj. *The Gospel of Mark*. Sacra Pagina. Collegeville: Liturgical Press, 2002.

Eckhart, Meister. "Be Still, and know that I am God (Psalm 46:10)." *Parabola* 33, no 1 (2008): 68–73.

Firth, David G. "Reading Psalm 46 in Its Canonical Context: An Initial Exploration in Harmonies Consonant and Dissonant." *Bulletin for Biblical Research* 30, no. 1 (2020): 22–40.

Fleming, David M. and Russell Fuller. "Book of Psalms." Pages 1313–15 in *Holman Illustrated Bible Dictionary*. Edited by Chad Brand. Nashville, TN: B&H, 2015.

Folger, Arie. "Understanding Psalm 46." *Jewish Bible Quarterly* 41, no. 1 (2013): 35–43.

Garland, David E. *Mark*. Grand Rapids, MI: Zondervan Academic, 1996.

Gault, Brian P. "Job's Hope: Redeemer or Retribution?" *Bibliotheca Sacra* 173, no. 690. (2016): 147–65.

Glaze, R. E. and Chad Brand. "Corinth." Pages 341–45 in *Holman Illustrated Bible Dictionary*. Edited by Chad Brand. Nashville, TN: B&H, 2015.

Glaze, R. E. and Chad Brand. "Second Letter to the Corinthians."
Pages 345–49 in *Holman Illustrated Bible Dictionary*. Edited
by Chad Brand. Nashville, Tennessee: B&H, 2015.

Green, Joel B. "Betwixt and Between: The Letter of James and the
Human Condition." *The Biblical Annals* 12, no. 2 (2022):
295–308.

Habito, Ruben. *Be Still and Know: Zen and the Bible*. Maryknoll,
NY: Orbis, 2017.

Hill, Andrew E. and John H. Walton. *A Survey of the Old Testament.*
Grand Rapids, MI: Zondervan Academic, 2009.

Jacobson, Rolf A. "Psalm 46: Translation, Structure, and Theology."
*Word & World* 40, no. 3 (2020): 308–20.

Keller, Timothy. *Walking with God Through Pain and Suffering*.
New York: Penguin, 2013.

Köstenberger, Andreas J., L. Scott Kellum, and Charles L. Quarles.
*The Lion and the Lamb: New Testament Essentials from the
Cradle, the Cross, and the Crown*. Brentwood, TN: B&H
Academic, 2012.

Kruse, Colin G. *2 Corinthians: An Introduction and Commentary*.
Nottingham: IVP Academic, 2015.

Kruse, Colin G., Andreas J. Köstenberger, and Robert W.
Yarbrough. *2 Corinthians*. Nashville, TN: B&H Academic,
2020.

Kynes, William Leland, and William Joseph Kynes. *Wrestling with
Job*. Downers Grove, IL: InterVarsity Press, 2022.

Kwon, JiSeong J. "Meaning and Context in Job and Tobit." *Journal for the Study of the Old Testament* 43, no. 4. (2019): 627–43.

Lepori, Mauro-Giuseppe. "Be Still and Know That I Am God." *The Tablet* 25 (2020): 8–10.

Lockett, Darian R. *Letters for the Church: Reading James, 1–2 Peter, 1–3 John, and Jude as Canon*. Westmont: InterVarsity Press, 2021.

Longman III, Tremper. *Introducing the Old Testament*. Grand Rapids, MI: Zondervan, 2012.

Martin, Ralph P. *2 Corinthians*. Grand Rapids, MI: Zondervan Academic, 2014.

McCartney, Dan G., Robert Yarbrough, and Robert Stein. *James*. Grand Rapids: Baker Academic, 2009.

Meek, Russell L. *Ecclesiastes: A Participatory Study Guide*. Gonzales, FL: Energion Publications, 2013.

Mitchell, Mike, and Phil Logan. "Korah." Page 979 in *Holman Illustrated Bible Dictionary*. Edited by Chad Brand. Nashville, TN: B&H, 2015.

Oden, Thomas C., and Christopher A. Hall, eds., *Mark: Volume 2*. Westmont: InterVarsity Press, 2005.

Patterson, Paige. "Letter from James." Pages 852–54 in *Holman Illustrated Bible Dictionary*. Edited by Chad Brand. Nashville, TN: B&H, 2015.

Peacock, Heber F., "Theology of the Gospel of Mark," *Review & Expositor* 55, no. 4 (1958): 393–399.

Reeves, Rodney. "Gospel of Mark." Pages 1055–57 in *Holman Illustrated Bible Dictionary*. Edited by Chad Brand. Nashville, TN: B&H, 2015.

Saint Nicodemus of the Holy Mountain. "Explanation of the Epistle of St. James." Translated Hieromonk (Papa) Ephraim. *The Orthodox Word* 58, no. 3 (2022): 105–142.

Stein, Robert H. *Mark (Baker Exegetical Commentary on the New Testament)*. Grand Rapids, MI: Baker Academic, 2008.

Telford, W. R. *The Theology of the Gospel of Mark*. Cambridge: Cambridge University Press, 1999.

Theodoret of Cyrus. *Commentary on the Psalms, Psalms 1–72*. Washington, D. C.: Catholic University of America Press.

Thomas, John Christopher. "'An Angel from Satan': Paul's Thorn in the Flesh (2 Corinthians 12:7-10)." *Journal of Pentecostal Theology* 4, no. 9 (1996): 39–52.

Vicchio, Stephen J. *The Book of Job: A History of Interpretation and a Commentary*. Eugene, OR: Wipf & Stock, 2020.

Ware, Archimandrite Kallistos. "Be Still, and Know That I Am God (Psalm 46:10)." *Parabola* 33, no 1 (2008): 68–73.

Warren, Bill. "John Mark." Page 1057 in *Holman Illustrated Bible Dictionary*. Edited by Chad Brand. Nashville, TN: B&H, 2015.

Wilson, Lindsay. *Job*. Grand Rapids, MI: Eerdmans, 2015.

Wolmarans, J. L. P. "Making Sense out of Suffering: James 1:2–4."
*HTS Teologiese Studies/ Theological Studies* 47, no. 4
(1991):1109–1122.

# About The Author

Suzanne Stucky brings together an unwavering devotion to Jesus, a biblical education, and over forty years of progressive health struggles. Her powerful testimony makes her a relatable example of the intersection of suffering and faith. Hers is a story of perseverance through trials.

After earning her Master of Business Administration (MBA) degree and working in the fields of marketing, sales, graphic design and advertising, she had to stop working in order to take care of her declining health. Unsure of her purpose, Suzanne then walked through life trying to survive her multiple diseases until God led her to further her biblical knowledge by obtaining her Master of Arts in Biblical Studies (MABS) degree. When God called, Suzanne responded, and her purpose became clear: to share her journey through declining health and her unwavering faith in God, offering hope and encouragement to others as they navigate their own struggles. The result is *When Will the Suffering End?*

Born and raised in Los Angeles, California, Suzanne now resides in Reno, Nevada with her husband of over thirty-five years and their two huge dogs. They live just a few miles from their only daughter and her family, and together, they all attend church in Reno. Who would have thought, but this California girl loves the snow.

To contact Suzanne Stucky, email at stuckybooks@gmail.com.

9 798234 046659